Contents

Animal Planet 2

Celebration Cupcakes 18

Princess Power.................................34

Just Plain Fun.................................48

Fruit Follies 66

Cha-Cha Chocolate.........................80

Animal Planet

Mini Mice

1 package (about 18 ounces) chocolate cake mix, plus ingredients to prepare mix
1 container (16 ounces) chocolate frosting
1 container (16 ounces) white frosting
Small black and pink hard candies or decors
Small fruit-flavored pastel candy wafers
Black string licorice

1. Preheat oven to 350°F. Line 60 mini (1¾-inch) muffin cups with paper baking cups.

2. Prepare cake mix according to package directions. Spoon batter into prepared muffin cups, filling almost full.

3. Bake 12 minutes or until toothpick inserted into centers comes out clean. Cool in pans 10 minutes. Remove to wire racks; cool completely.

4. For brown mice, frost cupcakes with chocolate frosting; use knife or small spatula to pull up frosting and create fuzzy appearance. For speckled mice, frost cupcakes with white frosting; use toothpick to add streaks of chocolate frosting.

5. Arrange candies on one side of each cupcake for eyes, nose and ears. Cut licorice into 3-inch lengths; press into opposite end of each cupcake for tail.

Makes 60 mini cupcakes

Dinocakes

1 package (about 18 ounces) chocolate fudge or devil's food cake mix, plus ingredients to prepare mix
44 long chewy chocolate candies (3×¼ inch), divided
10 to 15 small chewy chocolate candies
1 container (16 ounces) chocolate frosting
Candy sprinkles and decorating decors

1. Preheat oven to 350°F. Line 22 standard (2½-inch) muffin cups with paper baking cups.

2. Prepare cake mix according to package directions. Spoon batter into prepared muffin cups, filling two-thirds full.

3. Bake 20 minutes or until toothpick inserted into centers comes out clean. Cool in pans 10 minutes. Remove to wire racks; cool completely.

4. Shape 22 long candies into dinosaur heads. (To soften candies for easier shaping, microwave on LOW (30%) 6 to 8 seconds.)

5. Cut about 1 inch from remaining 22 long candies with scissors; shape each into pointed tail. Make four to five small cuts along length of candies, being careful not to cut all the way through. Curve candies into tail shape. Press and flatten small candies into rectangles; cut rectangles into small triangles for dinosaur spikes.

6. Frost cupcakes. Press candy head and tail into opposite sides of each cupcake; arrange candy triangles in between. Decorate top with sprinkles; press decors into dinosaur heads for eyes.   *Makes 22 cupcakes*

Hedgehogs

1 package (about 18 ounces) chocolate cake mix, plus ingredients
    to prepare mix
1 container (16 ounces) chocolate frosting
    Black jelly beans
    Small round white candies
    Black decorating gel
    Candy-coated licorice pieces

1. Preheat oven to 350°F. Place 22 standard (2-inch) silicone muffin cups on baking sheet or line 22 standard (2½-inch) muffin cups with paper baking cups.

2. Prepare cake mix according to package directions. Spoon batter into prepared muffin cups, filling two-thirds full.

3. Bake 20 minutes or until toothpick inserted into centers comes out clean. If using pans, cool in pans 10 minutes. Remove to wire racks; cool completely.

4. Frost cupcakes. Cut jelly beans in half crosswise for noses. Arrange jelly bean halves and round candies on one side of each cupcake for faces; pipe dot of decorating gel onto each eye. Arrange licorice pieces around faces and all over each cupcake. *Makes 22 cupcakes*

 **Tip** Silicone muffin cups are available at many gourmet, craft and baking supply stores.

Colorful Caterpillar Cupcakes

> 1 package (about 18 ounces) vanilla cake mix
> 1¼ cups water
> 3 eggs
> ⅓ cup vegetable oil
> Assorted food coloring
> Buttercream Frosting (recipe follows)
> Assorted candies, candy-coated chocolate pieces, red string licorice, lollipops and gummy worms

1. Preheat oven to 350°F. Line 20 standard (2½-inch) muffin cups with paper baking cups. (Use white paper baking cups to best show colors of caterpillar.)

2. Beat cake mix, water, eggs and oil in large bowl with electric mixer at low speed 30 seconds. Beat at medium speed 2 minutes or until well blended. Divide batter among five bowls; add different food coloring to each bowl, a few drops at a time, until desired shades are reached. Spoon batter into prepared muffin cups, filling three-fourths full.

3. Bake 20 minutes or until toothpick inserted into centers comes out clean. Cool in pans 10 minutes. Remove to wire racks; cool completely.

4. Prepare Buttercream Frosting. Set aside two cupcakes for caterpillar head. Frost remaining cupcakes. Place one cupcake on its side at edge of serving plate. Place second cupcake on its side in front of first cupcake; arrange remaining cupcakes, alternating colors, in a row to create body of caterpillar.

5. Frost one reserved cupcake; decorate with assorted candies, chocolate pieces, licorice and lollipops for face. Place plain cupcake upright at front of cupcake row for head; top with face cupcake on its side. Cut gummy worms into small pieces; attach along caterpillar body with frosting for legs.

Makes 20 cupcakes

Buttercream Frosting: Beat 1 cup (2 sticks) softened unsalted butter, 1 teaspoon vanilla, 1 teaspoon orange extract and ¼ teaspoon salt in medium bowl with electric mixer at medium speed until fluffy. Beat in 1 tablespoon meringue powder and 1 tablespoon milk. Gradually add 1 package (16 ounces) powdered sugar, beating after each addition until blended. Beat 5 minutes or until light and fluffy.

Fishy Friends

1 package (about 18 ounces) cake mix, any flavor, plus ingredients
    to prepare mix
1 container (16 ounces) white frosting
  Orange, purple and blue food coloring
  Assorted colored jelly candy fruit slices
  White round candies
  Colored round gummy candies
  Black decorating gel

1. Preheat oven to 350°F. Line 22 standard (2½-inch) muffin cups with paper baking cups.

2. Prepare cake mix according to package directions. Spoon batter into prepared muffin cups, filling two-thirds full.

3. Bake 20 minutes or until toothpick inserted into centers comes out clean. Cool in pans 10 minutes. Remove to wire racks; cool completely.

4. Divide frosting among three small bowls. Add different food coloring to each bowl, a few drops at a time, until desired shades are reached. Frost cupcakes.

5. Cut jelly candies into triangles for fins and tails. Arrange white candies and gummy candies at one end of each cupcake for faces; pipe dot of decorating gel onto each eye. Arrange jelly candy triangles on top and side of each cupcake.

Makes 22 cupcakes

Turtle Treats

1 package (about 18 ounces) chocolate cake mix, plus ingredients to prepare mix
1½ packages (12 ounces each) small chewy chocolate candies
1 container (16 ounces) vanilla frosting
Green food coloring
Chocolate-covered raisins, chocolate chips or candy-coated chocolate pieces
White decorating decors

1. Preheat oven to 350°F. Line 20 standard (2½-inch) muffin cups with paper baking cups.

2. Prepare cake mix according to package directions. Spoon batter into prepared muffin cups, filling three-fourths full.

3. Bake 20 minutes or until toothpick inserted into centers comes out clean. Cool in pans 10 minutes. Remove to wire racks; cool completely.

4. For each turtle, cut 2 candies in half; shape pieces into feet. (To soften candies for easier shaping, microwave on LOW (30%) 6 to 8 seconds.) Shape 1 candy into turtle head. Stretch 1 candy into long thin rope; cut into ½-inch piece for tail. Set aside.

5. Remove paper baking cups; cut off ½ inch from bottom of each cupcake. Discard bottoms of cupcakes. Place frosting in small bowl. Add food coloring, a few drops at a time, until desired shade is reached. Frost cupcakes.

6. Press candy head and tail into opposite ends of each cupcake; arrange chocolate-covered raisins on top of frosting. Press decors into heads for eyes. Arrange 4 candy feet around each turtle.   *Makes 20 cupcakes*

Little Lamb Cakes

1 package (about 18 ounces) yellow cake mix, plus ingredients
    to prepare mix
1 container (16 ounces) vanilla frosting
15 large marshmallows
    Pink jelly beans or decorating candies
1 package (10½ ounces) mini marshmallows
    Black string licorice
44 mini chocolate chips

1. Preheat oven to 350°F. Line 22 standard (2½-inch) muffin cups with paper baking cups.

2. Prepare cake mix according to package directions. Spoon batter into prepared muffin cups, filling two-thirds full.

3. Bake 20 minutes or until toothpick inserted into centers comes out clean. Cool in pans 10 minutes. Remove to wire racks; cool completely.

4. Frost cupcakes. Cut each large marshmallow crosswise into three pieces. Stretch and flatten pieces into oval shapes; arrange on cupcakes to resemble ears. Using frosting, attach pink jelly bean to each ear.

5. Press mini marshmallows into frosting around edge of cupcakes. Cut jelly beans in half crosswise; cut licorice into ½-inch pieces. Create faces with mini chocolate chips for eyes, jelly bean halves for noses and licorice for mouths.

Makes 22 cupcakes

Panda Cupcakes

1 package (about 18 ounces) yellow cake mix, plus ingredients to prepare mix

1 container (16 ounces) vanilla frosting

44 large chocolate discs*

44 small chocolate nonpareil candies

8 ounces semisweet chocolate, chopped *or* 1½ cups semisweet chocolate chips

44 white candy sprinkles

22 red jelly beans

Chocolate discs are available at many gourmet, craft and baking supply stores. Large chocolate nonpareil candies may be substituted.

1. Preheat oven to 350°F. Line 22 standard (2½-inch) muffin cups with paper baking cups.

2. Prepare cake mix according to package directions. Spoon batter into prepared muffin cups, filling two-thirds full.

3. Bake 20 minutes or until toothpick inserted into centers comes out clean. Cool in pans 10 minutes. Remove to wire racks; cool completely.

4. Frost cupcakes. Arrange 2 chocolate discs on edge of each cupcake for ears. Using frosting, attach 1 nonpareil candy to each ear.

5. Place semisweet chocolate in small food storage bag. Microwave on HIGH 1½ minutes or until chocolate is melted, kneading bag every 30 seconds. Cut very small hole in corner of bag; pipe mouths with melted chocolate. Pipe kidney shapes for eyes. Place candy sprinkle on each eye. Place jelly beans between eyes for noses.   *Makes 22 cupcakes*

Celebration Cupcakes

Chocolate Sweetheart Cupcakes

1 package (about 18 ounces) chocolate cake mix, plus ingredients
   to prepare mix
1 container (16 ounces) vanilla frosting
3 tablespoons seedless raspberry jam

1. Preheat oven to 350°F. Line 24 standard (2½-inch) muffin cups with paper baking cups.

2. Prepare cake mix according to package directions. Spoon batter into prepared muffin cups, filling two-thirds full.

3. Bake 20 minutes or until toothpick inserted into centers comes out clean. Cool in pans 10 minutes. Remove to wire racks; cool completely.

4. Combine frosting and jam in medium bowl. Cut off rounded tops of cupcakes with serrated knife. Cut out heart shape from each cupcake top with mini cookie cutter; discard cutouts.

5. Spread frosting mixture generously over cupcake bottoms, mounding slightly in center. Replace cupcake tops, pressing gently to fill hearts with frosting mixture.

Makes 24 cupcakes

Easy Easter Cupcakes

  1 package (about 18 ounces) yellow cake mix, plus ingredients
     to prepare mix
  1 container (16 ounces) vanilla frosting
    Green food coloring
24 sugar-coated colored marshmallow chicks and/or rabbits
    Round white candies

1. Preheat oven to 350°F. Line 24 standard (2½-inch) muffin cups with paper baking cups.

2. Prepare cake mix according to package directions. Spoon batter into prepared muffin cups, filling two-thirds full.

3. Bake 20 minutes or until toothpick inserted into centers comes out clean. Cool in pans 10 minutes. Remove to wire racks; cool completely.

4. Place frosting in small bowl. Add food coloring, a few drops at a time, until desired shade is reached. Frost cupcakes.

5. Trim marshmallow animals with scissors or knife to fit on cupcakes. Place one marshmallow on each cupcake. Decorate edges of cupcakes with white candies.

Makes 24 cupcakes

 Tip

Make a colorful batch of these cupcakes by using different shades of frosting, a variety of colored marshmallows and different colored candies.

Chocolate Easter Baskets

1 package (about 18 ounces) chocolate cake mix, plus ingredients to prepare mix
22 long chewy chocolate candies (3×¼ inches)
   Colored candy dots or decors (optional)
1 container (16 ounces) chocolate frosting
   Edible Easter grass (see Note)
   Candy-coated chocolate eggs, gumdrops or jelly beans

1. Preheat oven to 350°F. Line 22 standard (2½-inch) muffin cups with paper baking cups.

2. Prepare cake mix according to package directions. Spoon batter into prepared muffin cups, filling two-thirds full.

3. Bake 20 minutes or until toothpick inserted into centers comes out clean. Cool in pans 10 minutes. Remove to wire racks; cool completely.

4. For each basket handle, stretch or roll 1 candy between hands to 6-inch length. (To soften candies for easier shaping, microwave on LOW (30%) 6 to 8 seconds.) Shape into handle; pinch ends slightly to make them pointed. Using frosting, attach candy dots to handles, if desired. Place handles on waxed paper until set.

5. Frost cupcakes. Arrange basket handles on cupcakes. Place small mound of grass on top of each cupcake; top with chocolate eggs or other candies.

Makes 22 cupcakes

Note: Edible Easter grass can be found seasonally at some candy and specialty stores. If it is not available, substitute tinted coconut. To tint coconut, dilute a few drops of green food coloring with ½ teaspoon water in a large food storage bag. Add 1 to 1½ cups flaked coconut; seal the bag and shake well until the coconut is evenly coated. For a deeper color, add additional diluted food coloring and shake again.

Graduation Party Cupcakes

   1 package (about 18 ounces) white cake mix
1¼ cups water
   ⅓ cup vegetable oil
   3 egg whites
      Food coloring in school colors
   1 container (16 ounces) white frosting
22 chocolate squares
      Gummy candy strips
22 mini candy-coated chocolate pieces

1. Preheat oven to 325°F. Line 22 standard (2½-inch) muffin cups with paper baking cups.

2. Beat cake mix, water, oil and egg whites in large bowl with electric mixer at medium speed 2 minutes or until blended. Add one food coloring, a few drops at a time, until desired shade is reached. Spoon batter into prepared muffin cups, filling two-thirds full.

3. Bake 20 minutes or until toothpick inserted into centers comes out clean. Cool in pans 10 minutes. Remove to wire racks; cool completely.

4. Place frosting in small bowl. Add other food coloring, a few drops at a time, until desired shade is reached. Frost cupcakes.

5. Place chocolate square on top of each cupcake. Using frosting, attach candy strips for tassel and chocolate piece to square for button.

Makes 22 cupcakes

Surprise Package Cupcakes

1 package (about 18 ounces) cake mix, any flavor, plus ingredients
    to prepare mix
1 container (16 ounces) vanilla frosting
    Food coloring (optional)
    White decorating icing
72 chewy fruit squares
    Assorted colored decors

1. Preheat oven to 350°F. Spray 24 standard (2½-inch) muffin cups with nonstick cooking spray or line with paper baking cups.

2. Prepare cake mix according to package directions. Spoon batter into prepared muffin cups, filling two-thirds full.

3. Bake 20 minutes or until toothpick inserted into centers comes out clean. Cool in pans 10 minutes. Remove to wire racks; cool completely.

4. Place frosting in small bowl. Add food coloring, a few drops at a time, until desired shade is reached, if desired. Frost cupcakes.

5. Using icing, pipe ribbons on fruit squares to resemble wrapped presents. Place 3 candy presents on each cupcake. Decorate with decors.

Makes 24 cupcakes

 Tip You may use vanilla frosting instead of decorating icing for the ribbons, if desired. Place frosting in a small resealable bag and cut a small corner off the bottom of the bag with scissors.

Taffy Apple Cupcakes

1¾ cups all-purpose flour
1 teaspoon baking soda
1 teaspoon ground cinnamon
½ teaspoon salt
1 cup applesauce
¾ cup sugar
½ cup vegetable oil
1 egg
3 packages (14 ounces each) caramels
½ cup milk
30 wooden craft sticks
2¼ cups chopped roasted peanuts

1. Preheat oven to 350°F. Spray 30 mini (1¾-inch) muffin cups with nonstick cooking spray or line with paper baking cups.

2. Whisk flour, baking soda, cinnamon and salt in medium bowl. Combine applesauce, sugar, oil and egg in large bowl. Add flour mixture; stir until blended. Spoon batter into prepared muffin cups, filling three-fourths full.

3. Bake 15 minutes or until toothpick inserted into centers comes out clean. Cool in pans 5 minutes. Remove to wire racks; cool completely.

4. Line baking sheet with waxed paper; spray with nonstick cooking spray. Place peanuts on plate or in shallow dish. Insert craft sticks into tops of cupcakes.

5. Place unwrapped caramels and milk in large microwavable bowl; microwave on HIGH 2 to 3 minutes or until melted and smooth, stirring after each minute. Working with one at a time, hold cupcake over bowl and spoon caramel over cupcake, rotating until completely coated. Immediately roll in peanuts to coat, pressing to adhere. Stand cupcake on prepared baking sheet. (Caramel may need to be reheated briefly if it becomes too thick.) Let stand 20 minutes or until set. *Makes 30 mini cupcakes*

Note: For a quicker version of this recipe, simply drizzle melted caramel over the cooled cupcakes and sprinkle with chopped peanuts.

Pumpkin Spice Cupcakes

1½ cups sugar
¾ cup (1½ sticks) unsalted butter, softened
3 eggs
1 can (15 ounces) solid-pack pumpkin
1 cup buttermilk
3 cups all-purpose flour
1 tablespoon baking powder
2 teaspoons ground cinnamon
1½ teaspoons baking soda
½ teaspoon salt
¼ teaspoon ground allspice
¼ teaspoon ground nutmeg
⅛ teaspoon ground ginger
Maple Frosting (recipe follows)
Colored decors or sugar (optional)

1. Preheat oven to 350°F. Line 24 standard (2½-inch) muffin cups with paper baking cups.

2. Beat sugar and butter in large bowl with electric mixer at medium speed 3 minutes or until light and fluffy. Add eggs, one at a time, beating well after each addition. Combine pumpkin and buttermilk in medium bowl; mix well. Whisk flour, baking powder, cinnamon, baking soda, salt, allspice, nutmeg and ginger in separate medium bowl. Alternately add flour mixture and pumpkin mixture to butter mixture, beating well after each addition. Spoon batter into prepared muffin cups, filling two-thirds full.

3. Bake 20 minutes or until toothpick inserted into centers comes out clean. Cool in pans 10 minutes. Remove to wire racks; cool completely. Prepare Maple Frosting; frost cupcakes. Sprinkle with decors, if desired.

Makes 24 cupcakes

Maple Frosting: Beat ¾ cup (1½ sticks) softened butter in large bowl with electric mixer at medium speed until light and fluffy. Add 3 tablespoons maple syrup and ½ teaspoon vanilla; beat until well blended. Gradually add 3½ cups powdered sugar, beating until light and fluffy. Add 1 to 2 tablespoons milk to reach desired spreading consistency, if necessary. Makes 2½ cups.

Sweet Snowmen

- 1 package (about 18 ounces) vanilla cake mix, plus ingredients to prepare mix
- 1 container (16 ounces) white frosting
- 22 standard marshmallows
- 1 package (7 ounces) flaked coconut
- 44 large black gumdrops
  - Mini orange candy-coated chocolate pieces
  - Mini semisweet chocolate chips
  - Round green gummy candies
  - Red pull-apart licorice twists

1. Preheat oven to 350°F. Line 22 standard (2½-inch) muffin cups with paper baking cups.

2. Prepare cake mix according to package directions. Spoon batter into prepared muffin cups, filling two-thirds full.

3. Bake 20 minutes or until toothpick inserted into centers comes out clean. Cool in pans 10 minutes. Remove to wire racks; cool completely.

4. Frost cupcakes. Place 1 marshmallow on each cupcake for head, arranging slightly off center. Lightly press coconut into frosting around marshmallow.

5. For each hat, press 1 gumdrop on work surface or between hands to flatten into 2-inch circle. Using frosting, attach second gumdrop, flat side down, to center of flattened gumdrop. Attach hats to tops of marshmallows.

6. Cut chocolate pieces in half with sharp knife. Using frosting, attach chocolate chips for eyes, orange chocolate pieces for noses and gummy candies for buttons. Separate licorice twists into 2-string pieces; cut into 6- to 8-inch lengths and tie around bottom of marshmallows to create scarves.

Makes 22 cupcakes

Princess Power

Fairy Tale Cupcakes

1 package (about 18 ounces) cake mix, any flavor, plus ingredients
    to prepare mix
1 container (16 ounces) white frosting
    Pink, purple, blue and yellow food coloring
    Silver dragées
    Assorted decors

1. Preheat oven to 350°F. Line 22 standard (2½-inch) muffin cups with paper baking cups or spray with nonstick cooking spray.

2. Prepare cake mix according to package directions. Spoon batter into prepared muffin cups, filling two-thirds full.

3. Bake 20 minutes or until toothpick inserted into centers comes out clean. Cool in pans 10 minutes. Remove to wire racks; cool completely.

4. Divide frosting between four bowls; add different food coloring to each bowl, a few drops at a time, until desired shades are reached. Frost cupcakes with pink, purple and blue frosting; smooth tops with small spatula.

5. Spoon yellow frosting into pastry bag with round decorating tip or small resealable food storage bag with small corner cut off. Pipe crowns and wands on cupcakes; decorate with dragées and decors. *Makes 22 cupcakes*

Friendly Frogs

1 package (about 18 ounces) cake mix, any flavor, plus ingredients
  to prepare mix
1 container (16 ounces) white frosting
  Green food coloring
  Green decorating sugar (optional)
  Black round candies or candy-coated chocolate pieces
  White chocolate candy discs
  Black and red string licorice
  Green jelly candy fruit slices (optional)

1. Preheat oven to 350°F. Line 22 standard (2½-inch) muffin cups with paper baking cups.

2. Prepare cake mix according to package directions. Spoon batter into prepared muffin cups, filling two-thirds full.

3. Bake 20 minutes or until toothpick inserted into centers comes out clean. Cool in pans 10 minutes. Remove to wire racks; cool completely.

4. Place frosting in small bowl. Add food coloring, a few drops at a time, until desired shade is reached. Frost cupcakes. Sprinkle with decorating sugar, if desired.

5. Using frosting, attach black candies to white discs for eyes. Cut licorice into shorter lengths for mouths and noses. Arrange candies on cupcakes for faces.

6. Use scissors to cut jelly candies into feet shapes, if desired. Place cupcakes on candy feet just before serving. *Makes 22 cupcakes*

Marshmallow Delights

2 cups all-purpose flour
1 teaspoon baking soda
1 teaspoon baking powder
½ teaspoon salt
½ cup sour cream
½ cup milk
1 teaspoon vanilla
1 cup granulated sugar
½ cup (1 stick) butter, softened
2 eggs
1½ cups white frosting
Green food coloring
Green decorating sugar (optional)
3 cups fruit-flavored mini marshmallows

1. Preheat oven to 350°F. Line 12 standard (2½-inch) muffin cups with paper baking cups.

2. Sift flour, baking soda, baking powder and salt into medium bowl. Combine sour cream, milk and vanilla in small bowl.

3. Beat granulated sugar and butter in large bowl with electric mixer at medium speed 2 minutes or until fluffy. Add eggs, one at a time, beating well after each addition. Beat in flour mixture alternately with sour cream mixture, beginning and ending with flour mixture. Spoon batter into prepared muffin cups.

4. Bake 20 minutes or until toothpick inserted into centers comes out clean. Cool in pan 10 minutes. Remove to wire rack; cool completely.

5. Place frosting in small bowl. Add food coloring, a few drops at a time, until desired shade is reached. Frost cupcakes. Sprinkle with decorating sugar, if desired. Arrange marshmallows over top of cupcakes. *Makes 12 cupcakes*

Under the Sea

1 package (about 18 ounces) cake mix, any flavor, plus ingredients to prepare mix
2 containers (16 ounces each) white frosting, divided
Blue, green, yellow, red and purple food coloring
White decorating sugar (optional)
Black decorating gel
Assorted color decors, nonpareils and candy fish

1. Preheat oven to 350°F. Line 22 standard (2½-inch) muffin cups with paper baking cups.

2. Prepare cake mix according to package directions. Spoon batter into prepared muffin cups, filling three-fourths full.

3. Bake 20 minutes or until toothpick inserted into centers comes out clean. Cool in pans 10 minutes. Remove to wire racks; cool completely.

4. Place one container of frosting in small bowl; add blue and green food coloring, a few drops at a time, until desired shade of aqua is reached. Spoon frosting into pastry bag fitted with large star tip. Pipe frosting in swirl pattern on cupcakes. Sprinkle with decorating sugar, if desired.

5. Divide remaining frosting among four bowls; add different food colorings (except blue) to each bowl, a few drops at a time, until desired shades are reached. Spoon each color into pastry bag fitted with small round tip or resealable food storage bags with small corner cut off. Pipe yellow fish, red crabs, purple starfish and green seaweed on cupcakes. Pipe eyes with decorating gel and decorate with decors, nonpareils and candies.

Makes 22 cupcakes

Pretty in Pink

        2 cups all-purpose flour
        1 teaspoon baking soda
        1 teaspoon baking powder
    ½ teaspoon salt
    ½ cup sour cream
    ½ cup milk
        1 teaspoon vanilla
        1 cup granulated sugar
    ½ cup (1 stick) butter, softened
        2 eggs
        2 to 3 tablespoons multi-colored cake sprinkles
        1 container (16 ounces) white frosting
            Pink food coloring
            White and pink decorating sugars
    12 small tiaras

1. Preheat oven to 350°F. Line 12 standard (2½-inch) muffin cups with paper baking cups.

2. Sift flour, baking soda, baking powder and salt into medium bowl. Combine sour cream, milk and vanilla in small bowl until well blended.

3. Beat granulated sugar and butter in large bowl with electric mixer at medium speed 2 minutes or until fluffy. Add eggs, one at a time, beating well after each addition. Beat in flour mixture alternately with sour cream mixture, beginning and ending with flour mixture. Stir in sprinkles until blended. Spoon batter into prepared muffin cups.

4. Bake 20 minutes or until toothpick inserted into centers comes out clean. Cool in pan 10 minutes. Remove to wire rack; cool completely.

5. Place frosting in small bowl. Add food coloring, a few drops at a time, until desired shade is reached. Frost cupcakes. Sprinkle with decorating sugars; arrange tiaras on tops of cupcakes.   *Makes 12 cupcakes*

Dragonflies

1 package (about 18 ounces) cake mix, any flavor, plus ingredients to prepare mix

White confectionery coating*

Pink, purple, yellow and green food coloring

44 small pretzel twists

22 (2½-inch) pretzel sticks

White and purple nonpareils

Silver dragées

1 container (16 ounces) white frosting

Confectionery coating, also called almond bark or candy coating, can be found at craft stores and in the baking section of the supermarket. It comes in blocks, discs and chips and is usually available in white, milk and dark chocolate varieties.

1. Preheat oven to 350°F. Line 22 standard (2½-inch) muffin cups with paper baking cups.

2. Prepare cake mix according to package directions. Spoon batter into prepared muffin cups, filling two-thirds full.

3. Bake 20 minutes or until toothpick inserted into centers comes out clean. Cool in pans 10 minutes. Remove to wire racks; cool completely.

4. Line baking sheet with waxed paper. Melt confectionery coating according to package directions. Stir in pink food coloring, a few drops at a time, until desired shade is reached. Dip pretzel twists in melted coating; arrange two twists together on prepared baking sheet. Dip pretzel sticks in coating; place one stick between two pretzel twists to create dragonfly. Sprinkle pretzel twists with white nonpareils; arrange two purple nonpareils at top of pretzel sticks for eyes. Press dragées into bottom half of pretzel sticks. Let stand 10 minutes or until set.

5. Meanwhile, divide frosting among three small bowls. Add different food coloring (except pink) to each bowl, a few drops at a time, until desired shades are reached. Frost cupcakes. Top with dragonflies.

Makes 22 cupcakes

Angelic Cupcakes

1 package (about 16 ounces) angel food cake mix
1¼ cups cold water
¼ teaspoon peppermint extract (optional)
Red food coloring
4½ cups frozen whipped topping, thawed

1. Preheat oven to 375°F. Line 36 standard (2½-inch) muffin cups with paper baking cups.

2. Beat cake mix, water and peppermint extract, if desired, in large bowl with electric mixer at low speed 2 minutes. Pour half of batter into medium bowl. Add food coloring, a few drops at a time, until desired shade is reached. Alternately spoon half of white and pink batters into each prepared muffin cup, filling three-fourths full.

3. Bake 11 minutes or until cupcakes are golden brown with deep cracks on top. Cool in pans 10 minutes. Remove to wire racks; cool completely.

4. Divide whipped topping between two small bowls. Add food coloring to one bowl, a few drops at a time, until desired shade is reached. Frost cupcakes with pink and white whipped topping. *Makes 36 cupcakes*

 Tip Be sure to thaw whipped topping in the refrigerator, not at room temperature, so that it will not make the frosting runny.

Just Plain Fun

Sunny Side Upcakes

1 package (about 18 ounces) vanilla cake mix, plus ingredients
   to prepare mix
22 yellow chewy fruit candy squares
2 containers (16 ounces each) white frosting

1. Preheat oven to 350°F. Line 22 standard (2½-inch) muffin cups with paper baking cups.

2. Prepare cake mix according to package directions. Spoon batter into prepared muffin cups, filling two-thirds full.

3. Bake 20 minutes or until toothpick inserted into centers comes out clean. Cool in pans 10 minutes. Remove to wire racks; cool completely.

4. For each egg yolk, unwrap 1 candy square and microwave on LOW (30%) 5 seconds or just until softened. Shape into ball; flatten slightly.

5. Place 1 cup frosting in small microwavable bowl; microwave on LOW (30%) 10 seconds or until softened. Working with one cupcake at a time, spoon about 2 tablespoons frosting in center of top of cupcake. Spread frosting toward edges of cupcake in uneven petal shape to resemble egg white. Press candy into frosting in center of cupcake to resemble yolk. Microwave additional frosting as needed.

Makes 22 cupcakes

Red Velvet Cupcakes

2¼ cups all-purpose flour
1 teaspoon salt
2 bottles (1 ounce each) red food coloring
3 tablespoons unsweetened cocoa powder
1 cup buttermilk
1 teaspoon vanilla
1½ cups sugar
½ cup (1 stick) unsalted butter, softened
2 eggs
1 teaspoon white vinegar
1 teaspoon baking soda
1 to 2 containers (16 ounces each) whipped cream cheese frosting
Toasted coconut* (optional)

To toast coconut, spread evenly on ungreased baking sheet. Bake in preheated 350°F oven 5 to 7 minutes or until light golden brown, stirring occasionally.

1. Preheat oven to 350°F. Line 18 standard (2½-inch) muffin cups with paper baking cups.

2. Combine flour and salt in medium bowl. Gradually stir food coloring into cocoa in small bowl until blended and smooth. Combine buttermilk and vanilla in another small bowl.

3. Beat sugar and butter in large bowl with electric mixer at medium speed 4 minutes or until light and fluffy. Add eggs, one at a time, beating well after each addition. Add cocoa mixture; beat until well blended and uniform in color. Add flour mixture alternately with buttermilk mixture, beating just until blended. Whisk vinegar into baking soda in small bowl; gently fold into batter with spatula or spoon (do not use mixer). Spoon batter into prepared muffin cups, filling two-thirds full.

4. Bake 20 minutes or until toothpick inserted into centers comes out clean. Cool in pans 10 minutes. Remove to wire racks; cool completely.

5. Frost cupcakes. Sprinkle with coconut, if desired.   *Makes 18 cupcakes*

Margarita Cupcakes

1 package (about 18 ounces) white cake mix
¾ cup plus 2 tablespoons margarita mix, divided
2 eggs
⅓ cup vegetable oil
¼ cup water
3 teaspoons grated lime peel, divided
Juice of 1 lime
2 tablespoons tequila
3 cups powdered sugar
1 tablespoon white decorating sugar or granulated sugar
1 tablespoon salt
Green and yellow food coloring
Lime peel strips (optional)

1. Preheat oven to 350°F. Line 24 standard (2½-inch) muffin cups with paper baking cups.

2. Beat cake mix, ¾ cup margarita mix, eggs, oil, water, 1 teaspoon lime peel and lime juice in large bowl with electric mixer at medium speed until well blended. Spoon batter into prepared muffin cups.

3. Bake 20 minutes or until toothpick inserted into centers comes out clean. Cool in pans 10 minutes. Remove to wire racks; cool completely.

4. Combine tequila, remaining 2 tablespoons margarita mix and 2 teaspoons lime peel in medium bowl. Gradually stir in powdered sugar. Combine decorating sugar and salt in small bowl. Add food coloring, one drop at a time, until desired shade is reached.

5. Spread glaze over cupcakes; roll edges in sugar-salt mixture. Garnish with lime peel strips.

Makes 24 cupcakes

Cupcake Sliders

      2 cups all-purpose flour
2½ teaspoons baking powder
   ½ teaspoon salt
      1 cup milk
   ½ teaspoon vanilla
1½ cups sugar
   ½ cup (1 stick) butter, softened
      3 eggs
1¼ cups chocolate hazelnut spread or milk chocolate frosting
         Colored decors (optional)

1. Preheat oven to 350°F. Spray 18 standard (2½-inch) muffin cups with nonstick cooking spray.

2. Combine flour, baking powder and salt in medium bowl. Combine milk and vanilla in small bowl. Beat sugar and butter in large bowl with electric mixer at medium speed 3 minutes or until creamy. Add eggs, one at a time, beating well after each addition. Add flour mixture alternately with milk mixture, beating until well blended. Spoon batter into prepared muffin cups, filling three-fourths full.

3. Bake 20 minutes or until toothpick inserted into centers comes out clean. Cool in pans 10 minutes. Remove to wire racks; cool completely.

4. Cut off edges of cupcakes to form squares. Cut cupcakes in half crosswise. Spread each bottom half with 1 tablespoon chocolate hazelnut spread; sprinkle with decors. Replace tops of cupcakes.   *Makes 18 cupcakes*

Marshmallow Fudge Sundae Cupcakes

1 package (about 18 ounces) chocolate cake mix, plus ingredients
    to prepare mix
2 packages (4 ounces each) waffle bowls
40 large marshmallows
1 jar (8 ounces) hot fudge topping
    Colored sprinkles or chopped nuts
1¼ cups whipped topping
1 jar (10 ounces) maraschino cherries

1. Preheat oven to 350°F. Spray 20 standard (2½-inch) muffin cups with nonstick cooking spray.

2. Prepare cake mix according to package directions. Spoon batter into prepared muffin cups, filling two-thirds full.

3. Bake 20 minutes or until toothpick inserted into centers comes out clean. Cool in pans 10 minutes. Remove to wire racks; cool completely.

4. Place waffle bowls on ungreased baking sheets. Place one cupcake in each waffle bowl. Top each cupcake with 2 marshmallows; bake 2 minutes or until marshmallows are slightly softened.

5. Remove lid from hot fudge topping; microwave on HIGH 10 seconds or until softened. Top each cupcake with hot fudge topping, sprinkles, whipped topping and 1 cherry.   *Makes 20 cupcakes*

 **Tip** Make your favorite type of sundae by substituting caramel ice cream topping or strawberry sauce for the hot fudge topping.

Cookie in a Cupcake

1 package (16 ounces) refrigerated break-apart chocolate chip cookie dough (24 count)
4 cups all-purpose flour
1 cup unsweetened cocoa powder
2 teaspoons baking soda
1 teaspoon salt
1 cup (2 sticks) butter, softened
2 cups sugar
2 eggs
2 teaspoons vanilla
1 cup sour cream
1 cup hot water

1. Preheat oven to 350°F. Place 24 standard (2-inch) silicone muffin cups on baking sheet or line 24 standard (2½-inch) muffin cups with paper baking cups.

2. Break apart dough into 24 pieces along score lines. Roll each piece of dough into ball; refrigerate dough while preparing cupcake batter.

3. Sift flour, cocoa, baking soda and salt into medium bowl. Beat butter in large bowl with electric mixer 2 minutes or until creamy. Add sugar; beat 2 minutes or until light and fluffy. Beat in egg until well blended. Beat in vanilla.

4. Add sour cream and water to butter mixture alternately with flour mixture, beginning and ending with flour mixture. Beat until well blended. Spoon batter into prepared muffin cups. Place 1 ball of cookie dough into each cup, pressing down into batter.

5. Bake 20 minutes or until toothpick inserted into cake portion of cupcake comes out clean. Cool in pan 10 minutes. Remove to wire rack to cool slightly. Serve warm.

Makes 24 cupcakes

Peanut Butter & Jelly Cupcakes

1 package (about 18 ounces) yellow cake mix, plus ingredients
to prepare mix
2 cups strawberry jelly
¾ cup creamy peanut butter
½ cup (1 stick) butter, softened
2 cups powdered sugar
½ teaspoon vanilla
¼ cup milk

1. Preheat oven to 350°F. Line 22 standard (2½-inch) muffin cups with paper baking cups.

2. Prepare cake mix according to package directions. Spoon batter into prepared muffin cups, filling two-thirds full.

3. Bake 20 minutes or until toothpick inserted into centers comes out clean. Cool in pans 10 minutes. Remove to wire racks; cool completely.

4. Place jelly in pastry bag fitted with small round tip. Insert tip into tops of cupcakes; squeeze bag gently to fill centers with jelly.

5. Beat peanut butter and butter in medium bowl with electric mixer at medium speed 2 minutes or until smooth. Add powdered sugar and vanilla; beat at low speed 1 minute or until crumbly. Gradually beat in milk until creamy. Frost cupcakes.   *Makes 22 cupcakes*

Hot Chocolate Cupcakes

1 package (about 16 ounces) pound cake mix, plus ingredients
    to prepare mix
4 containers (4 ounces each) prepared chocolate pudding*
2½ cups whipped topping, divided
4 small chewy chocolate candies
    Unsweetened cocoa powder

*Or prepare 1 package (4-serving size) instant chocolate pudding and pie filling mix according to package directions. Use 2 cups pudding for recipe; reserve remaining pudding for another use.

1. Preheat oven to 350°F. Spray 15 standard (2½-inch) muffin cups with baking spray (nonstick cooking spray with flour added) or grease and flour cups.

2. Prepare cake mix according to package directions. Spoon batter into prepared muffin cups, filling two-thirds full.

3. Bake 20 minutes or until toothpick inserted into centers comes out clean. Cool in pans 10 minutes. Remove to wire racks; cool completely.

4. Combine chocolate pudding and 2 cups whipped topping in medium bowl until well blended. Cover and refrigerate until ready to use.

5. Working with one at a time, stretch chocolate candies into long thin rope; cut ropes into 2-inch lengths. (To soften candies for easier shaping, microwave on LOW (30%) 6 to 8 seconds.) Curve candy pieces into handles for mugs.

6. Cut 2-inch hole from top of each cupcake with small paring knife. Cut two slits, ½ inch apart, in one side of each cupcake. Insert chocolate candy into slits for mug handles. Fill in hole and top of each cupcake with chocolate pudding mixture. Top with small dollop of remaining whipped topping; sprinkle with cocoa.

Makes 15 cupcakes

Mini Doughnut Cupcakes

1 cup sugar
1½ teaspoons ground cinnamon
1 package (about 18 ounces) yellow or white cake mix, plus ingredients to prepare mix
1 tablespoon ground nutmeg

1. Preheat oven to 350°F. Grease and flour 60 mini (1¾-inch) muffin cups. Combine sugar and cinnamon in small bowl; set aside.

2. Prepare cake mix according to package directions; stir in nutmeg. Spoon batter into prepared muffin cups, filling two-thirds full.

3. Bake 12 minutes or until lightly browned and toothpick inserted into centers comes out clean.

4. Remove cupcakes from pans. Roll warm cupcakes in sugar mixture until completely coated. Serve warm or cool completely on wire racks.

Makes 60 mini cupcakes

Tip

These irresistible little cupcakes allow you to enjoy the lightly spiced flavor of your favorite donuts without all the time and mess it takes to prepare and fry them at home.

Fruit Follies

Key Lime Pie Cupcakes

  1 package (about 18 ounces) lemon cake mix with pudding in the mix
  1 cup vegetable oil
  4 eggs
  ¾ cup key lime juice,* divided
  ½ cup water
  1 teaspoon grated lime peel
  2 cups whipping cream
  ½ cup powdered sugar
     Lime wedges or additional grated lime peel (optional)

If you cannot find key lime juice, you may substitute with regular lime juice.

1. Preheat oven to 350°F. Line 24 standard (2½-inch) muffin cups with paper baking cups.

2. Beat cake mix, oil, eggs, ½ cup key lime juice, water and lime peel in large bowl 2 minutes or until thick and smooth. Spoon batter into prepared muffin cups, filling two-thirds full.

3. Bake 20 minutes or until toothpick inserted into centers comes out clean. Cool in pans 10 minutes. Remove to wire racks; cool completely.

4. Beat cream in medium bowl with electric mixer at medium speed 3 to 5 minutes or until soft peaks form. Add powdered sugar and remaining ¼ cup key lime juice; beat at medium-high speed 30 seconds or until medium-stiff peaks form.

5. Top each cupcake with whipped cream. Garnish with lime wedges. Serve immediately.   *Makes 24 cupcakes*

Blueberry Cheesecake Cupcakes

1 package (about 16 ounces) refrigerated mini break-apart sugar cookie dough (40 count)
2 packages (8 ounces each) cream cheese, softened
1 cup sugar
2 eggs
1 tablespoon cornstarch
1½ teaspoons vanilla
3 egg whites
½ teaspoon cream of tartar
¼ cup blueberry preserves
1 pint fresh blueberries (optional)

1. Preheat oven to 325°F. Line 20 standard (2½-inch) muffin cups with foil baking cups; spray with nonstick cooking spray.

2. Break off 2 cookie pieces from refrigerated dough. Roll pieces into ball, flatten slightly and press into bottom of one baking cup. Repeat with remaining cookie dough.

3. Bake 10 minutes. Remove from oven and immediately press down center of each cookie with back of spoon.

4. Beat cream cheese in large bowl with electric mixer at medium speed until smooth. Add sugar, eggs, cornstarch and vanilla; beat until smooth and well blended. Set aside.

5. Beat egg whites and cream of tartar in medium bowl with electric mixer at high speed until stiff peaks form. Stir half of egg white mixture into cream cheese mixture. Gently fold in remaining egg white mixture just until combined. Gently stir in blueberry preserves. Spoon batter over cooled cookie cups.

6. Bake 17 to 20 minutes. (Centers will be spongy to the touch). Cool in pans 10 minutes. Cool completely in pans in refrigerator. Garnish with blueberries.

Makes 20 cupcakes

Note: It is important to use foil baking cups because they provide extra structure for the cheesecake.

•Fruit Follies•

Banana Cupcakes

2 cups all-purpose flour
1½ cups granulated sugar
2 tablespoons packed brown sugar
2 teaspoons baking powder
½ teaspoon salt
½ teaspoon ground cinnamon
¼ teaspoon ground allspice
½ cup vegetable oil
2 eggs
¼ cup milk
1 teaspoon vanilla
2 mashed bananas (about 1 cup)
1 container (16 ounces) chocolate frosting
Chocolate sprinkles (optional)

1. Preheat oven to 350°F. Line 18 standard (2½-inch) muffin cups with paper baking cups.

2. Combine flour, granulated sugar, brown sugar, baking powder, salt, cinnamon and allspice in large bowl. Add oil, eggs, milk and vanilla; beat with electric mixer at medium speed 2 minutes or until well blended. Beat in bananas until well blended. Spoon batter into prepared muffin cups, filling three-fourths full.

3. Bake 25 minutes or until toothpick inserted into centers comes out clean. Cool in pans 10 minutes. Remove to wire racks; cool completely.

4. Frost cupcakes; decorate with sprinkles, if desired.   *Makes 18 cupcakes*

Pink Lemonade Cupcakes

1 package (about 18 ounces) white cake mix without pudding in the mix
1 cup water
3 egg whites
⅓ cup plus ¼ cup frozen pink lemonade concentrate, divided
2 tablespoons vegetable oil
  Red food coloring, divided
4 cups powdered sugar
⅓ cup butter, softened
  Lemon slice candies (optional)

1. Preheat oven to 350°F. Line 24 standard (2½-inch) muffin cups with paper baking cups.

2. Beat cake mix, water, egg whites, ⅓ cup lemonade concentrate, oil and a few drops food coloring in large bowl with electric mixer at medium speed 2 minutes or until well blended. (Add additional food coloring, a few drops at a time, until desired shade is reached.) Spoon batter into prepared muffin cups.

3. Bake 20 minutes or until toothpick inserted into centers comes out clean. Cool in pans 10 minutes. Remove to wire racks; cool completely.

4. Beat powdered sugar, butter and remaining ¼ cup lemonade concentrate in medium bowl with electric mixer at medium speed until well blended. Add food coloring, a few drops at a time, until desired shade is reached. Frost cupcakes. Garnish with candies.

Makes 24 cupcakes

Raspberry Streusel Cupcakes

    Streusel Topping (recipe follows)
 3 cups all-purpose flour
 2 teaspoons baking powder
 ½ teaspoon salt
 ⅛ teaspoon ground cinnamon
 1½ cups sugar
 ½ cup (1 stick) butter, softened
 2 eggs
 1 teaspoon vanilla
 1 cup sour cream
 1½ pints fresh raspberries

1. Preheat oven to 350°F. Line 24 standard (2½-inch) muffin cups with paper baking cups. Prepare Streusel Topping; set aside.

2. Whisk flour, baking powder, salt and cinnamon in medium bowl. Beat sugar and butter in large bowl with electric mixer at medium speed 2 to 3 minutes or until light and fluffy. Add eggs, one at a time, beating well after each addition. Stir in vanilla. Add flour mixture alternately with sour cream, beating just until blended. Gently fold in raspberries. Spoon into prepared muffin cups; sprinkle with Streusel Topping.

3. Bake 20 minutes or until toothpick inserted into centers comes out clean. Cool in pans 10 minutes. Remove to wire racks; cool completely.

Makes 24 cupcakes

Streusel Topping: Combine 1 cup sugar, ⅔ cup all-purpose flour, ¼ cup pecan chips, 1 teaspoon ground cinnamon and ¼ teaspoon salt in medium bowl. Cut ½ cup (1 stick) butter into small pieces; cut butter and 1 tablespoon milk into sugar mixture with pastry blender or two knives until mixture resembles coarse crumbs.

Lemon Meringue Cupcakes

1 package (about 18 ounces) lemon cake mix, plus ingredients
    to prepare mix
¾ cup prepared lemon curd*
4 egg whites
6 tablespoons sugar

Lemon curd, a thick sweet lemon spread, is available in many supermarkets near the jams and preserves.

1. Preheat oven to 350°F. Line 9 jumbo (3½-inch) muffin cups with paper baking cups.

2. Prepare cake mix according to package directions. Spoon batter into prepared muffin cups, filling two-thirds full.

3. Bake 20 minutes or until toothpick inserted into centers comes out clean. Cool in pans 10 minutes. Remove to wire racks; cool completely. *Increase oven temperature to 375°F.*

4. Cut off tops of cupcakes with serrated knife. (Do not remove paper baking cups.) Scoop out small hole in center of each cupcake with tablespoon; fill each with 1 tablespoon lemon curd. Replace cupcake tops.

5. Beat egg whites in medium bowl with electric mixer at high speed until soft peaks form. Gradually add sugar, beating until stiff peaks form. Pipe or spread meringue in peaks on each cupcake.

6. Place cupcakes on baking sheet. Bake 5 minutes or until peaks of meringue are golden. *Makes 9 jumbo cupcakes*

Variation: This recipe can also be used to make 24 standard (2½-inch) cupcakes. Line muffin pans with paper baking cups. Prepare and bake cake mix according to package directions. Cut off tops of cupcakes; scoop out hole in each cupcake with teaspoon and fill each with 1 teaspoon lemon curd. Pipe or spread meringue in peaks on each cupcake; bake as directed above.

Strawberry Short Cupcakes

2 cups all-purpose flour
2½ teaspoons baking powder
½ teaspoon salt
1 cup milk
1 teaspoon vanilla
1½ cups plus 3 tablespoons sugar, divided
½ cup (1 stick) butter, softened
3 eggs
1½ cups cold whipping cream
2 quarts fresh strawberries, sliced

1. Preheat oven to 350°F. Spray 18 standard (2½-inch) muffin cups with nonstick cooking spray.

2. Combine flour, baking powder and salt in medium bowl. Combine milk and vanilla in small bowl. Beat 1½ cups sugar and butter in large bowl with electric mixer at medium speed 3 minutes or until creamy. Add eggs, one at a time, beating well after each addition. Add flour mixture alternately with milk mixture, beating until well blended. Spoon batter into prepared muffin cups, filling three-fourths full.

3. Bake 20 minutes or until toothpick inserted into centers comes out clean. Cool in pans 10 minutes. Remove to wire racks; cool completely.

4. Beat cream in large bowl with electric mixer at high speed until soft peaks form. Gradually add remaining 3 tablespoons sugar; beat until stiff peaks form.

5. Cut cupcakes in half crosswise. Top each bottom half with about 2 tablespoons whipped cream and strawberries. Replace top half; top with additional whipped cream and strawberries. *Makes 18 cupcakes*

Cha-Cha Chocolate

Chocolate Hazelnut Cupcakes

1¾ cups all-purpose flour
1½ teaspoons baking powder
½ teaspoon salt
2 cups chocolate hazelnut spread, divided
⅓ cup (⅔ stick) butter, softened
¾ cup sugar
2 eggs
1 teaspoon vanilla
1¼ cups milk
Chopped hazelnuts (optional)

1. Preheat oven to 350°F. Line 18 standard (2½-inch) muffin cups with paper or foil baking cups.

2. Whisk flour, baking powder and salt in medium bowl. Beat ⅓ cup chocolate hazelnut spread and butter in large bowl with electric mixer at medium speed until smooth. Beat in sugar until well blended. Beat in eggs and vanilla. Add flour mixture alternately with milk, beginning and ending with flour mixture, beating until blended. Spoon batter into prepared muffin cups, filling two-thirds full.

3. Bake 20 minutes or until toothpick inserted into centers comes out clean. Cool in pans 10 minutes. Remove to wire racks; cool completely.

4. Spread remaining 1⅔ cups chocolate hazelnut spread on top of cupcakes. Sprinkle with hazelnuts, if desired.

Makes 18 cupcakes

Mini Turtle Cupcakes

1 package (21½ ounces) brownie mix plus ingredients to prepare mix
½ cup chopped pecans
1 container (16 ounces) dark chocolate frosting
½ cup coarsely chopped pecans, toasted
12 caramels
1 to 2 tablespoons whipping cream

1. Preheat oven to 350°F. Line 54 mini (1½-inch) muffin cups with paper baking cups.

2. Prepare brownie mix according to package directions. Stir in ½ cup chopped pecans. Spoon batter into prepared muffin cups, filling two-thirds full.

3. Bake 18 minutes or until toothpick inserted into centers comes out clean. Cool in pans 5 minutes. Remove to wire racks; cool completely.

4. Frost cupcakes; top with ½ cup toasted pecans.

5. Combine caramels and 1 tablespoon cream in small saucepan over low heat; cook and stir until caramels are melted and mixture is smooth. Add additional 1 tablespoon cream to thin mixture, if necessary. Spoon caramel over cupcakes. Store at room temperature up to 24 hours or cover and refrigerate up to 3 days. *Makes 54 mini cupcakes*

Tip

To toast pecans, spread in single layer on ungreased baking sheet. Bake in preheated 350°F oven 8 to 10 minutes or until golden brown, stirring frequently.

Classic Chocolate Cupcakes

1¾ cups all-purpose flour
1¼ cups sugar
2 teaspoons baking powder
½ teaspoon salt
¾ cup *each* vegetable oil and milk
3 eggs
1½ teaspoons vanilla
8 squares (1 ounce each) semisweet chocolate, melted and cooled slightly
Chocolate Buttercream Frosting (recipe follows)
Colored sprinkles (optional)

1. Preheat oven to 350°F. Line 20 standard (2½-inch) muffin cups with paper baking cups.

2. Whisk flour, sugar, baking powder and salt in large bowl. Add oil, milk, eggs and vanilla; beat with electric mixer at medium speed 2 minutes or until well blended. Stir in melted chocolate until well blended. Spoon batter into prepared muffin cups, filling three-fourths full. Bake 20 minutes or until toothpick inserted into centers comes out clean. Cool in pans 10 minutes. Remove to wire racks; cool completely.

3. Prepare Chocolate Buttercream Frosting; frost cupcakes. Decorate with sprinkles, if desired. *Makes 20 cupcakes*

Chocolate Buttercream Frosting

4 cups powdered sugar, sifted, divided
¾ cup butter, softened
6 squares (1 ounce each) unsweetened chocolate, melted
6 to 8 tablespoons milk, divided
¾ teaspoon vanilla

Beat 2 cups powdered sugar, butter, chocolate, 4 tablespoons milk and vanilla in large bowl with electric mixer at medium speed until smooth. Add remaining 2 cups sugar; beat until fluffy. Add additional milk, 1 tablespoon at a time, to reach desired spreading consistency, if necessary. *Makes about 3 cups*

•Cha-Cha Chocolate•

Mini Tiramisu Cupcakes

2 teaspoons instant espresso powder
1 tablespoon hot water
1 tablespoon coffee liqueur
1 package (about 18 ounces) butter recipe yellow cake mix
3 eggs
⅔ cup water
½ cup (1 stick) butter, softened and cut into small pieces
1 package (8 ounces) mascarpone cheese*
½ cup powdered sugar
¼ teaspoon vanilla
½ (8-ounce) container French vanilla whipped topping
Unsweetened cocoa powder

Mascarpone cheese is an Italian soft cheese (similar to cream cheese) that is a traditional ingredient in tiramisu. Look for it in the specialty cheese section of the supermarket.

1. Preheat oven to 350°F. Line 18 standard (2½-inch) muffin cups with paper baking cups.

2. Whisk espresso powder into hot water in medium bowl until dissolved. Stir in liqueur. Beat cake mix, eggs, water and butter in large bowl with electric mixer at medium speed 3 minutes or until smooth. Combine half of batter with coffee mixture; mix well. Spoon equal amounts of coffee batter and plain batter into each prepared muffin cup, filling three-fourths full. Swirl batters with toothpick or paring knife.

3. Bake 16 minutes or until toothpick inserted into centers comes out clean. Cool in pans 10 minutes. Remove to wire racks; cool completely.

4. Combine mascarpone cheese, powdered sugar and vanilla in medium bowl. Fold in whipped topping.

5. Cut off tops of cupcakes with serrated knife. Cut out designs from center of each cupcake top with mini cookie cutters. Discard cutouts.

6. Spoon filling evenly over cupcake bottoms. Sprinkle cupcake tops with cocoa; place over filling. Refrigerate 2 hours before serving.

Makes 18 cupcakes

Rocky Road Cupcakes

1 package (about 18 ounces) chocolate fudge cake mix
1⅓ cups water
3 eggs
½ cup vegetable oil
¾ cup mini semisweet chocolate chips, divided
1 container (16 ounces) chocolate frosting
1 cup mini marshmallows
⅔ cup walnut pieces
Hot fudge ice cream topping or chocolate syrup, heated

1. Preheat oven to 325°F. Line 22 standard (2½-inch) muffin cups with paper baking cups.

2. Beat cake mix, water, eggs, oil and ¼ cup chocolate chips in large bowl with electric mixer at low speed 30 seconds. Beat at medium speed 2 minutes or until well blended. Spoon batter into prepared muffin cups, filling two-thirds full.

3. Bake 20 minutes or until toothpick inserted into centers comes out clean. Cool in pans 10 minutes. Remove to wire racks; cool completely.

4. Spread thin layer of frosting over cupcakes. Top with marshmallows, walnuts and remaining ½ cup chocolate chips, pressing down lightly to adhere to frosting. Drizzle with hot fudge topping. *Makes 22 cupcakes*

 *Tip* To heat hot fudge topping, remove lid and microwave on HIGH 10 seconds or until softened.

Black Bottom Cupcakes

1 package (8 ounces) cream cheese, softened
4 eggs, divided
½ cup plus ⅓ cup granulated sugar, divided
2 cups all-purpose flour
1 cup packed brown sugar
¾ cup unsweetened cocoa powder
1 teaspoon baking powder
½ teaspoon baking soda
½ teaspoon salt
1 cup buttermilk
½ cup vegetable oil
1½ teaspoons vanilla

1. Preheat oven to 350°F. Line 20 standard (2½-inch) muffin cups with paper or foil baking cups.

2. Beat cream cheese, 1 egg and ⅓ cup granulated sugar in small bowl until smooth and creamy. Set aside.

3. Whisk flour, brown sugar, cocoa, remaining ½ cup granulated sugar, baking powder, baking soda and salt in large bowl. Beat buttermilk, remaining 3 eggs, oil and vanilla in medium bowl until blended. Add buttermilk mixture to flour mixture; beat 2 minutes or until well blended.

4. Spoon batter into prepared muffin cups, filling about three-fourths full. Spoon heaping tablespoon cream cheese mixture over batter in each cup; gently swirl with tip of knife.

5. Bake 20 minutes or until toothpick inserted into centers comes out clean. Cool in pans 10 minutes. Remove to wire racks; cool completely.

Makes 20 cupcakes

•Cha-Cha Chocolate•

Fudgy Mocha Cupcakes with Chocolate Coffee Ganache

1 package (about 18 ounces) devil's food cake mix without pudding in the mix
1 package (4-serving size) chocolate fudge instant pudding and pie filling mix
1⅓ cups strongly brewed coffee, at room temperature
3 eggs
½ cup vegetable oil
6 ounces semisweet chocolate, finely chopped
½ cup whipping cream
2 teaspoons instant coffee granules
½ cup prepared white frosting

1. Preheat oven to 350°F. Line 18 standard (2½-inch) muffin cups with paper baking cups.

2. Beat cake mix, pudding mix, coffee, eggs and oil in large bowl with electric mixer at medium speed 2 minutes until well blended. Spoon batter into prepared muffin cups, filling two-thirds full.

3. Bake 20 minutes or until toothpick inserted into centers comes out clean. Cool in pans 10 minutes. Remove to wire racks; cool completely.

4. Place chocolate in small bowl. Heat cream and instant coffee in small saucepan over medium-low heat until bubbles appear around edge of pan. Pour cream over chocolate; let stand 2 minutes. Stir until mixture is smooth and shiny. Cool completely. (Ganache will be slightly runny.)

5. Dip tops of cupcakes into ganache, smoothing surface with back of spoon. Place frosting in pastry bag fitted with small round writing tip. Pipe letters onto cupcakes.

Makes 18 cupcakes

S'more-Topped Cupcakes

1¼ cups all-purpose flour
½ cup unsweetened cocoa powder
¾ teaspoon baking soda
½ teaspoon salt
½ cup (1 stick) butter, softened
1¼ cups sugar
2 eggs
1 cup milk
1 teaspoon vanilla
6 whole graham crackers (12 squares)
1½ cups marshmallow creme
1½ bars (3 to 4 ounces each) milk chocolate, chopped into ½-inch chunks

1. Preheat oven to 350°F. Line 12 standard (2½-inch) muffin cups with paper baking cups.

2. Sift flour, cocoa, baking soda and salt into medium bowl. Beat butter in large bowl with electric mixer at medium speed until creamy. Add sugar; beat 3 minutes. Add eggs, one at a time, beating well after each addition. Combine milk and vanilla in small bowl. Beat in flour mixture and milk mixture alternately to batter, beginning and ending with flour mixture. Spoon batter into prepared muffin cups, filling three-fourths full.

3. Bake 20 minutes or until toothpick inserted into centers comes out clean. Cool in pan 10 minutes. Remove to wire rack; cool completely.

4. Break each graham cracker square into ¾-inch pieces; press onto each cupcake to completely cover top and extend slightly over edge of cupcake. Spread 2 tablespoons marshmallow creme over each cupcake (see Note); top with chocolate chunks. Freeze 15 minutes or until set.

5. Preheat broiler. Place cupcakes on baking sheet. Broil 6 inches from heat source 1 minute or until marshmallow creme is lightly browned. Serve immediately.

Makes 12 cupcakes

Note: Marshmallow creme is very sticky and can be difficult to spread. Spray your utensils with nonstick cooking spray; drop teaspoon-size dollops of marshmallow creme over graham crackers and spread gently to cover.

•Cha-Cha Chocolate•

Double Malted Cupcakes

  2 cups all-purpose flour
  ¼ cup plus 1 tablespoon malted milk powder, divided
  2 teaspoons baking powder
  ¼ teaspoon salt
  1¾ cups granulated sugar
  ¾ cup (1½ sticks) butter, softened, divided
  1 cup milk
  2½ teaspoons vanilla, divided
  3 egg whites
  4 ounces milk chocolate candy bar, broken into chunks
  ¼ cup whipping cream
  1¾ cups powdered sugar
  30 chocolate-covered malt ball candies

1. Preheat oven to 350°F. Line 30 standard (2½-inch) muffin cups with paper baking cups.

2. Whisk flour, ¼ cup malted milk powder, baking powder and salt in medium bowl. Beat granulated sugar and ½ cup butter in large bowl with electric mixer at medium speed 1 minute. Add milk and 1½ teaspoons vanilla; beat at low speed 30 seconds. Gradually add flour mixture; beat at medium speed 2 minutes. Add egg whites; beat 1 minute. Spoon batter into prepared muffin cups, filling two-thirds full.

3. Bake 20 minutes or until toothpick inserted into centers comes out clean. Cool in pans 10 minutes. (Centers of cupcakes will sink slightly upon cooling.) Remove to wire racks; cool completely.

4. Melt chocolate and remaining ¼ cup butter in medium heavy saucepan over low heat, stirring frequently. Stir in cream, remaining 1 tablespoon malted milk powder and 1 teaspoon vanilla. Gradually stir in powdered sugar. Cook and stir until smooth. Remove from heat. Refrigerate 20 minutes, beating every 5 minutes or until frosting is of spreading consistency.

5. Frost cupcakes; top with malt ball candies. Store at room temperature up to 24 hours or refrigerate up to 3 days.   *Makes 30 cupcakes*

•Cha-Cha Chocolate•

Contents

Adorable Animals 98

Just For Kids....................114

Fun & Games....................130

Favorite Foods....................146

Let's Celebrate 162

Cookie Creations....................178

Adorable Animals

Cookie Dough Bears

1 package (about 16 ounces) refrigerated sugar cookie dough
1 cup quick oats
    Mini semisweet chocolate chips

1. Let dough stand at room temperature 15 minutes. Combine dough and oats in medium bowl; beat with electric mixer at medium speed until blended. Cover and freeze 15 minutes.

2. Preheat oven to 350°F. Lightly coat cookie sheets with nonstick cooking spray. For each bear, shape 1 (1-inch) ball for body and 1 (¾-inch) ball for head. Place body and head together on cookie sheets; flatten slightly. Form 7 small balls for arms, legs, ears and nose; arrange on bear body and head. Place 2 chocolate chips on each head for eyes. Place 1 chocolate chip on each body for belly button.

3. Bake 12 minutes or until edges are lightly browned. Cool on cookie sheets 2 minutes. Remove to wire racks; cool completely.   *Makes about 9 cookies*

Tasty Turtles

 3½ cups all-purpose flour
  ½ teaspoon salt
 1½ cups sugar
   1 cup (2 sticks) unsalted butter, softened
   2 eggs
   2 teaspoons vanilla
     Green gel food coloring
 144 green gumdrops
     Green, black and red decorating gels
     Brown candy-coated chocolate pieces
     Brown mini candy-coated chocolate pieces

1. Whisk flour and salt in medium bowl. Beat sugar and butter in large bowl with electric mixer at medium speed until light and fluffy. Add eggs, one at a time, beating until blended after each addition. Add vanilla; beat until blended.

2. Gradually add flour mixture, beating until blended after each addition. Add food coloring, a few drops at a time, to dough; beat until evenly colored. Divide dough evenly into 2 discs. Wrap and refrigerate 1 hour.

3. Preheat oven to 350°F. Line cookie sheets with parchment paper. Working with 1 disc at a time, cut each disc into 36 equal pieces. Roll each piece into a ball; flatten slightly. Place 1 inch apart on prepared cookie sheets. Refrigerate 15 minutes.

4. Bake 12 minutes or until set. Cool on cookie sheets 5 minutes. Remove to wire racks; cool completely.

5. Reserve 72 gumdrops. Cut remaining gumdrops into quarters. Dot backs of gumdrop pieces with green decorating gel and adhere to sides of cookies for legs. Dot bottoms of reserved gumdrops with green decorating gel and adhere 1 to each cookie for head. Dot backs of 3 chocolate pieces with green decorating gel and adhere to center of each cookie. Dot backs of mini chocolate pieces with green decorating gel and adhere to create remainder of shell.

6. Pipe eyes, nose and mouth on each head using black and red decorating gels. Let stand 10 minutes or until set.   *Makes 6 dozen cookies*

•Adorable Animals•

Zebras

2 packages (about 16 ounces each) refrigerated sugar cookie dough
½ cup all-purpose flour
½ cup unsweetened Dutch process cocoa powder*
Prepared dark chocolate frosting
Assorted sprinkles
Mini semisweet chocolate chips and semisweet chocolate chips

Dutch process, or European-style, cocoa powder gives these cookies an intense chocolate flavor and a dark, rich color. Other unsweetened cocoa powders can be substituted, but the flavor may be milder and the color may be lighter.

1. Let doughs stand at room temperature 15 minutes.

2. Combine 1 package dough and flour in large bowl; beat with electric mixer at medium speed until well blended. Combine remaining package dough and cocoa in another large bowl; beat at medium speed until well blended. Form each dough into disc; wrap and freeze 15 minutes.

3. Working with 1 disc at a time, roll out dough between parchment paper into 9-inch square. Place cocoa dough on top of plain dough. Cut into 4 (4½-inch) squares. Layer squares on top of each other, alternating cocoa and plain doughs. Wrap and refrigerate 4 hours or up to 2 days.

4. Preheat oven to 350°F. Lightly grease cookie sheets. Trim edges of dough to make square, if necessary. Cut dough into ¼-inch striped slices, wiping off knife after each cut; cut slices in half to make 2¼×2-inch rectangles. Place rectangles 2 inches apart on prepared cookie sheets.

5. Working with stripes vertically, cut small triangle from top left corner and narrow triangle from top right edge of each rectangle. Discard scraps. Cut small triangle from center of bottom edge; place at top of cookie for ear.

6. Bake 10 minutes or until edges are light brown. Cool on cookie sheets 5 minutes. Remove to wire racks; cool completely.

7. For manes, spread frosting on cookie edges at both sides of ear; top with sprinkles. Attach mini chocolate chips to each cookie with frosting for eye and nostril.

Makes about 3 dozen cookies

Peppermint Pigs

1 package (about 16 ounces) refrigerated sugar cookie dough
½ cup all-purpose flour
¾ teaspoon peppermint extract
Red food coloring
White decorating icing
Mini candy-coated chocolate pieces

1. Let dough stand at room temperature 15 minutes. Lightly grease cookie sheets.

2. Preheat oven to 350°F. Combine dough, flour, peppermint extract and food coloring in large bowl; beat with electric mixer at medium speed until well blended. Divide dough into 20 equal pieces.

3. Shape each dough piece into 1 (1-inch) ball, 1 (½-inch) ball and 2 (¼-inch) balls. Flatten 1-inch ball into ¼-inch-thick circle; place on prepared cookie sheets. Flatten ½-inch ball into ¼-inch-thick oval; place on top of circle for snout. Shape 2 (¼-inch) balls into triangles; fold point over and place at top of circle for ears. Make indentations in snout with toothpick for nostrils.

4. Bake 10 minutes or until set. Cool on cookie sheets 2 minutes. Remove to wire racks; cool completely. Pipe 2 small circles on each face with white decorating icing. Press chocolate pieces into icing for eyes.

Makes 20 cookies

 **Tip** You may substitute pink gel food coloring, if desired. Gels are more concentrated, so you can use less and still get dynamic colors. You can find a wide selection of gel food colorings at craft or specialty kitchen stores or online.

Panda Pals

3½ cups all-purpose flour
1 teaspoon salt
1½ cups sugar
1 cup (2 sticks) unsalted butter, softened
2 eggs
1 teaspoon *each* almond extract and vanilla
1 cup prepared white or vanilla frosting
Black gel food coloring
Black jelly beans, cut in half

1. Whisk flour and salt in medium bowl. Beat sugar and butter in large bowl with electric mixer at medium speed until light and fluffy. Add eggs, one at a time, beating until blended after each addition. Add almond extract and vanilla; beat until blended.

2. Gradually add flour mixture, beating until blended after each addition. Divide dough evenly into 2 discs. Wrap and refrigerate 1 hour.

3. Preheat oven to 350°F. Line cookie sheets with parchment paper. Working with 1 disc at a time, roll out dough between parchment paper to ⅜-inch thickness. From each disc, cut out 6 large circles with 3-inch round cookie cutter, 6 medium circles with 1¾-inch round cookie cutter and 12 small circles with 1¼-inch round cookie cutter.

4. Place large circles 3 inches apart on prepared cookie sheets. Place 2 small circles next to each large circle for ears. Place medium circles 1 inch apart on separate prepared cookie sheet. Refrigerate 15 minutes.

5. Bake large circles 15 minutes or until set. Bake medium circles 12 minutes or until set. Cool on cookie sheets 5 minutes. Remove to wire racks; cool completely.

6. Spread medium circles with frosting; spread thin layer of frosting on backs and adhere to large circles for mouths. Add food coloring, a few drops at a time, to remaining frosting; stir until evenly colored. Spread small circles with black frosting for ears. Dot cut side of jelly beans with frosting and adhere for eyes and noses. Pipe mouth using black frosting. Let stand 10 minutes or until set.

Makes 1 dozen cookies

Citrus Easter Chicks

1 package (about 16 ounces) refrigerated sugar cookie dough
⅓ cup all-purpose flour
1 teaspoon lemon extract
Lemon Cookie Glaze (recipe follows)
2 cups shredded coconut, tinted yellow*
Mini semisweet chocolate chips, assorted candies and decors

*To tint coconut, combine small amount of food coloring (paste or liquid) with 1 teaspoon water in large bowl. Add coconut and stir until evenly coated. Add more food coloring, if needed.

1. Let dough stand at room temperature 15 minutes.

2. Combine dough, flour and lemon extract in large bowl; beat with electric mixer at medium speed until well blended. Divide dough evenly into 2 discs. Wrap and refrigerate 1 hour.

3. Preheat oven to 350°F. Working with 1 disc at a time, roll out dough between parchment paper to ¼-inch thickness. Cut out shapes with 2- to 3-inch chick cookie cutters. Place 2 inches apart on ungreased cookie sheets.

4. Bake 7 minutes or until set. Cool on cookie sheets 5 minutes. Remove to wire racks; cool completely.

5. Place wire racks over parchment paper. Prepare Lemon Cookie Glaze; spread over cookies. Sprinkle with coconut. Decorate chicks with mini chocolate chips, candies and decors as desired. Let stand 40 minutes or until set.

Makes about 1½ dozen cookies

Lemon Cookie Glaze

4 cups powdered sugar
½ teaspoon lemon peel
4 to 6 tablespoons lemon juice
Yellow food coloring

Combine powdered sugar, lemon peel and lemon juice, 1 tablespoon at a time, in medium bowl to make pourable glaze. Add food coloring, a few drops at a time; stir until evenly colored.

Makes about 2 cups

Mischievous Monkeys

     3 cups all-purpose flour
     ½ cup unsweetened cocoa powder
     1 teaspoon salt
    1½ cups sugar
     1 cup (2 sticks) unsalted butter, softened
     2 eggs
     1 teaspoon vanilla
        Yellow gel food coloring
     1 cup prepared white or vanilla frosting
        Black string licorice
    20 brown candy-coated peanut butter candies

1. Whisk flour, cocoa and salt in medium bowl. Beat sugar and butter in large bowl with electric mixer at medium speed until light and fluffy. Add eggs, one at a time, beating until blended after each addition. Add vanilla; beat until blended. Gradually add flour mixture, beating until blended after each addition. Divide dough evenly into 2 discs. Wrap and refrigerate 1 hour.

2. Preheat oven to 350°F. Line cookie sheets with parchment paper. Working with 1 disc at a time, roll out dough between parchment paper to ⅜-inch thickness. From each disc, cut out 5 large circles with 3-inch round cookie cutter, 5 medium circles with 2-inch round cookie cutter and 10 small circles with 1½-inch round cookie cutter.

3. Place large circles 3 inches apart on prepared cookie sheets. Place 2 small circles next to each large circle for ears. Place medium circles 1 inch apart on separate prepared cookie sheet. Refrigerate 15 minutes. Bake large circles 15 minutes or until set. Bake medium circles 12 minutes or until set. Cool on cookie sheets 5 minutes. Remove to wire racks; cool completely.

4. Add food coloring, a few drops at a time, to frosting; stir until evenly colored. Spread medium circles with frosting. Let stand 10 minutes or until set. Spread thin layer of frosting on backs of medium circles and adhere to large circles for mouths. Cut lengths of licorice for noses and mouths; press into frosting. Spread small circle of frosting on inside of each small circle for ears. Dot backs of 2 candies with frosting; adhere to each large circle just above medium circle for eyes. Let stand 10 minutes or until set. *Makes 10 cookies*

•Adorable Animals•

Snickerpoodles

1 package (about 16 ounces) refrigerated sugar cookie dough
1 teaspoon ground cinnamon, divided
1 teaspoon vanilla
¼ cup sugar
  Semisweet chocolate chips and mini semisweet chocolate chips
  White and pink decorating icings

1. Let dough stand at room temperature 15 minutes. Lightly grease cookie sheets.

2. Preheat oven to 350°F. Combine dough, ½ teaspoon cinnamon and vanilla in large bowl; beat with electric mixer at medium speed until well blended. Combine sugar and remaining ½ teaspoon cinnamon in small bowl. For each poodle face, shape 1½ teaspoons dough into oval. Roll in cinnamon-sugar mixture; place on prepared cookie sheets.

3. For poodle ears, divide 1½ teaspoons dough in half; shape each half into teardrop shape. Roll in cinnamon-sugar mixture; place at either side of face.

4. For top of poodle head, shape scant teaspoon dough into oval. Roll in cinnamon-sugar mixture; place at top of face.

5. Bake 10 minutes or until edges are lightly browned. Immediately press 1 chocolate chip onto each face for nose. Cool on cookie sheets 2 minutes. Remove to wire racks; cool completely.

6. Pipe 2 small circles on each face with white decorating icing. Press mini chocolate chips into icing for eyes. Decorate as desired with white and pink icings.   *Makes about 2 dozen cookies*

Just For Kids

Magic Lightning Bolts

1 package (about 16 ounces) refrigerated sugar cookie dough
  Blue food coloring
1 cup prepared cream cheese frosting
  Blue crackling candy or blue decorating sugar

1. Grease cookie sheets. Reserve half of dough; wrap and refrigerate.

2. Roll out remaining half of dough between parchment paper to ¼-inch thickness. Cut into zigzag lightning shapes about ½ inch wide and 5½ inches long. Place 2 inches apart on prepared cookie sheets. Repeat with reserved dough and scraps. Refrigerate 1 hour.

3. Preheat oven to 350°F. Bake 5 minutes or until edges are lightly browned. Cool on cookie sheets 2 minutes. Remove to wire racks; cool completely.

4. Just before serving, add food coloring, a few drops at a time, to frosting; stir until well blended. Spread frosting on cookies. Sprinkle crackling candy over frosting.

Makes about 2 dozen cookies

Note: If using crackling candy, do not frost and decorate cookies in advance. Crackling candy begins to lose its popping quality when it is exposed to air and moisture.

Chocolate Railroad Cookies

  2 cups all-purpose flour
¾ cup sugar
½ cup unsweetened cocoa powder
⅛ teaspoon salt
  1 cup (2 sticks) unsalted butter, slightly softened, cut into ½-inch pieces

1. Line cookie sheets with parchment paper. Whisk flour, sugar, cocoa and salt in large bowl with electric mixer at low speed until well combined. With mixer running on low, add butter, 1 piece at a time, beating until mixture looks moist and crumbly.

2. Knead dough with hands until butter is well incorporated. Divide dough in half. Shape each half into rough square; wrap and refrigerate 30 minutes.

3. Let 1 square dough stand at room temperature 15 minutes. Roll out dough between parchment paper into 10×6-inch rectangle (about ¼ inch thick). Trim edges, reserving scraps.

4. To make rails, cut 2 (¼-inch-wide) strips from the 10-inch side of the rectangle. Place parallel to each other, ½ inch apart, on prepared cookie sheet.

5. To make ties, cut off 2 more ¼-inch-wide strips of dough. Cut each strip into 6 pieces (each about 1½ inches long). Press 9 evenly spaced ties across rails. Reserve remaining 3 ties.

6. Repeat with remaining dough and reserved scraps to create 6 more railroad tracks. Refrigerate 15 minutes.

7. Cut each whole track into 3 separate tracks (3 ties per track), creating 21 cookies. Arrange cookies ½ inch apart on prepared cookie sheets.

8. Preheat oven to 350°F. Repeat steps 3 through 7 with second dough square for a total of 42 cookies.

9. Bake 12 minutes or until set. Cool completely on cookie sheets.

Makes 42 cookies

Peanut Butter Aliens

1 package (about 16 ounces) refrigerated sugar cookie dough
½ cup creamy peanut butter
⅓ cup all-purpose flour
¼ cup powdered sugar
½ teaspoon vanilla
   Green decorating icing
1 cup strawberry jam

1. Let dough stand at room temperature 15 minutes. Grease cookie sheets.

2. Preheat oven to 350°F. Beat dough, peanut butter, flour, powdered sugar and vanilla in large bowl with electric mixer at medium speed until well blended. Reserve half of dough; wrap and refrigerate.

3. Roll out remaining dough between parchment paper to ¼-inch thickness. Cut out 14 circles with 3-inch round cookie cutter; pinch 1 side of each circle to make teardrop shape. Place 2 inches apart on prepared cookie sheets. Bake 12 minutes or until set. Cool on cookie sheets 2 minutes. Remove to wire racks; cool completely.

4. Roll out reserved dough between parchment paper to ¼-inch thickness. Cut out 14 circles with 3-inch round cookie cutter; pinch 1 side of each circle to form teardrop shape. Place 2 inches apart on prepared cookie sheets. Cut out 2 oblong holes for eyes. Make small slit for mouth. Bake 12 minutes or until set. Cool on cookie sheets 2 minutes. Remove to wire racks; cool completely.

5. Spread icing on cookies with faces; let stand 10 minutes or until set. Spread jam on uncut cookies. Top each jam-topped cookie with green face cookie.

Makes 14 sandwich cookies

Dinosaur Egg Cookies

1 cup (2 sticks) margarine or butter, softened
1 cup confectioners' sugar
1 egg
1 teaspoon vanilla
1½ cups all-purpose flour
1¼ cups QUAKER® Oats (quick or old fashioned, uncooked)
½ cup cornstarch
¼ teaspoon salt (optional)
24 assorted bite-size candies
   Colored sugar or candy sprinkles

1. Heat oven to 325°F. Beat margarine and sugar in large bowl with electric mixer until creamy. Add egg and vanilla; beat well. Combine flour, oats, cornstarch and salt, if desired, in medium bowl; mix well. Add to creamed mixture; mix well.

2. Shape rounded tablespoonfuls of dough into 1½-inch balls. Press candy piece into center of each ball; shape dough around candy so it is completely hidden. Lightly pinch one side of dough to form egg shape. Roll cookies in desired decorations until evenly coated. Place 2 inches apart on ungreased cookie sheets.

3. Bake 16 minutes or until cookies are set and lightly browned on bottom. Remove to wire rack; cool completely. Store tightly covered.

Makes 2 dozen cookies

Cheery Chocolate Animal Cookies

1⅔ cups (10-ounce package) REESE'S® Peanut Butter Chips
1 cup HERSHEY'S SPECIAL DARK® Chocolate Chips or HERSHEY'S
    Semi-Sweet Chocolate Chips
2 tablespoons shortening (do not use butter, margarine, spread or oil)
1 package (20 ounces) chocolate sandwich cookies
1 package (11 ounces) animal crackers

1. Line trays or cookie sheets with wax paper.

2. Combine peanut butter chips, chocolate chips and shortening in 2-quart glass measuring cup with handle. Microwave at MEDIUM (50%) 1½ to |2 minutes or until chips are melted and mixture is smooth when stirred. Using fork, dip each cookie into melted chip mixture; gently tap fork on side of cup to remove excess chocolate.

3. Place coated cookies on prepared trays; top each cookie with an animal cracker. Chill until chocolate is set, about 30 minutes. Store in airtight container in a cool, dry place. *Makes about 4 dozen cookies*

 Tip These indulgent delights are perfect when you want to pack a special treat for long car trips or bag lunches because the chocolate coating helps contain any crumbs.

Swashbuckling Pirates

3½ cups all-purpose flour
1 teaspoon salt
1½ cups sugar
1 cup (2 sticks) unsalted butter, softened
2 eggs
2 teaspoons vanilla
Royal Icing (recipe follows)
Pink, orange, yellow and red gel food colorings
Red string licorice, red candy-coated chocolate pieces, black
    decorating gel and mini semisweet chocolate chips

1. Whisk flour and salt in medium bowl. Beat sugar and butter in large bowl with electric mixer at medium speed until light and fluffy. Add eggs, one at a time, beating until blended after each addition. Add vanilla; beat until blended. Gradually add flour mixture, beating until blended after each addition. Divide dough evenly into 2 discs. Wrap and refrigerate 1 hour.

2. Preheat oven to 350°F. Line cookie sheets with parchment paper. Working with 1 disc at a time, roll out dough between sheets of parchment paper to ⅜-inch thickness. Cut out circles with 3¼-inch round cookie cutter. Place 1 inch apart on prepared cookie sheets. Refrigerate 15 minutes. Bake 15 minutes or until set. Cool on cookie sheets 5 minutes. Remove to wire racks; cool completely.

3. Prepare Royal Icing. Reserve one third of icing in small bowl. Add pink, orange and yellow food colorings, a few drops at a time, to remaining icing to create peach color; stir until evenly colored. Spread two thirds of each cookie with peach icing. Let stand until set.

4. Spread remaining one third of each cookie with reserved white icing. Cut licorice for edge of bandana and mouth; press into icing. Press chocolate pieces into white icing. Pipe eye patch using decorating gel. Pipe eye with white icing; press mini chocolate chip into center. Press mini chocolate chips into icing for mustache. Let stand until set.   *Makes about 1½ dozen cookies*

Royal Icing: Beat 4 cups powdered sugar, 6 tablespoons water and 3 tablespoons meringue powder in medium bowl with electric mixer at high speed until soft peaks form. Cover surface with plastic wrap until needed. Makes about 2 cups.

•Just For Kids•

Building Blocks

1 package (about 16 ounces) refrigerated cookie dough, any flavor
Powdered Sugar Glaze (recipe follows)
Assorted food colorings
Assorted small round gummy candies (about ¼ inch in diameter)

1. Let dough stand at room temperature 15 minutes. Grease 13×9-inch baking pan.

2. Preheat oven to 350°F. Press dough evenly into bottom of prepared pan. Score dough lengthwise and crosswise into 32 equal rectangles (about 2¼×1½ inches each). Freeze 10 minutes.

3. Bake 10 minutes. Re-score partially baked cookies. Bake 5 minutes or until edges are lightly browned and center is set. Cut through score marks to separate cookies. Cool in pan 10 minutes. Remove to wire rack; cool completely.

4. Prepare Powdered Sugar Glaze. Tint glaze with food colorings as desired.

5. Place wire racks over waxed paper. Spread glaze over tops and sides of cookies. Let stand 5 minutes. Attach 6 gummy candies to each cookie. Let stand 40 minutes or until set.   *Makes 32 cookies*

Powdered Sugar Glaze

2 cups powdered sugar
6 to 9 tablespoons whipping cream, divided

Combine powdered sugar and 6 tablespoons cream in medium bowl; whisk until smooth. Add remaining cream, 1 tablespoon at a time, to make pourable glaze.   *Makes about 1 cup*

Magic Number Cookies

3½ cups all-purpose flour
1 teaspoon salt
1½ cups sugar
1 cup (2 sticks) unsalted butter, softened
2 eggs
2 teaspoons vanilla
Fuchsia and teal gel food colorings

1. Whisk flour and salt in medium bowl. Beat sugar and butter in large bowl with electric mixer at medium speed until light and fluffy. Add eggs, one at a time, beating until blended after each addition. Add vanilla; beat until blended.

2. Gradually add flour mixture, beating until blended after each addition. Divide dough in half; place in separate medium bowls. Add fuchsia food coloring, a few drops at a time, to half of dough; beat until evenly colored. Add teal food coloring, a few drops at a time, to remaining half of dough; beat until evenly colored. Shape each half of dough into disc; wrap and refrigerate 1 hour.

3. Preheat oven to 350°F. Line cookie sheets with parchment paper. Working with 1 disc at a time, roll out dough between parchment paper to ⅜-inch thickness. Cut out stars with 4½-inch cookie cutter. Place 1 inch apart on prepared cookie sheets. Cut out number from center of each star using 2-inch cookie cutter. Transfer fuchsia numbers to teal stars and teal numbers to fuchsia stars. Refrigerate 15 minutes.

4. Bake 15 minutes or until set. Cool on cookie sheets 5 minutes. Remove to wire racks; cool completely.

Makes about 1 dozen cookies

Treasure Chests

1 package (about 19 ounces) brownie mix, plus ingredients to prepare mix
1 container (16 ounces) chocolate frosting
24 fudge-covered graham crackers
   Yellow decorating icing
   Mini candy-coated chocolate pieces
   Yellow decorating gel

1. Preheat oven to 350°F. Coat 9-inch square baking pan with nonstick cooking spray.

2. Prepare brownie mix according to package directions; pour batter into prepared pan. Bake 35 minutes or until toothpick inserted into center comes out clean. Cool completely in pan on wire rack. Cover; freeze 1 hour or overnight.

3. Run knife around edges of brownies. Place cutting board over baking pan; invert and let stand until brownies release from pan. Trim edges; discard. Cut into 24 rectangles.

4. Spread tops and sides of brownies with frosting. Let stand on wire racks 10 minutes or until set. Pipe lines on brownies and graham crackers with decorating icing to resemble chests.

5. Dot back of chocolate pieces with decorating gel; adhere on front half of brownie tops for treasure. Spread 1 edge of each graham cracker with frosting; adhere 1 graham cracker to back half of each brownie top so that it leans on chocolate pieces. Let stand 10 minutes or until set.

Makes 2 dozen brownies

Fun & Games

Flip-Flops

1 package (about 16 ounces) refrigerated break-apart sugar
   cookie dough (24 count)
1 container (16 ounces) white or vanilla frosting
   Assorted gel food colorings
   Red string licorice
   Edible cake decorations*
   Star-shaped candy sprinkles

Edible cake decorations are made from molded sugar. They can be found in the baking aisle at large supermarkets, party supply stores and craft stores.

1. Let dough stand at room temperature 5 minutes. Line cookie sheets with parchment paper.

2. Preheat oven to 325°F. Roll out dough between parchment paper to ¼-inch thickness. Cut out flip-flop shapes with sharp knife (approximately 3×1½-inch shapes). Place 2 inches apart on prepared cookie sheets. Refrigerate 15 minutes.

3. Bake 13 minutes or until set. Cool on cookie sheets 5 minutes. Remove to wire racks; cool completely.

4. Divide frosting evenly among small bowls and tint with food colorings to make desired colors. Spread cookies with frosting. Cut licorice for straps; press into frosting. Top with cake decorations. Decorate with candy sprinkles as desired. Let stand 10 minutes or until set.   *Makes about 20 cookies*

Go Fly a Kite Cookies

3½ cups all-purpose flour
1 teaspoon salt
1½ cups sugar
1 cup (2 sticks) unsalted butter, softened
2 eggs
2 teaspoons vanilla
Royal Icing (recipe follows)
Blue and green gel food colorings
Yellow decorating icing

1. Whisk flour and salt in medium bowl. Beat sugar and butter in large bowl with electric mixer at medium speed until light and fluffy. Add eggs, one at a time, beating until blended after each addition. Add vanilla; beat until blended.

2. Gradually add flour mixture, beating until blended after each addition. Divide dough evenly into 2 discs. Wrap and refrigerate 1 hour.

3. Preheat oven to 350°F. Line cookie sheets with parchment paper. Working with 1 disc at a time, roll out dough between parchment paper to ⅜-inch thickness. Cut out circles with 3¼-inch round cookie cutter. Place 1 inch apart on prepared cookie sheets. Refrigerate 15 minutes. Bake 15 minutes or until set. Cool on cookie sheets 5 minutes. Remove to wire racks; cool completely.

4. Prepare Royal Icing. Reserve ¾ cup Royal Icing in medium bowl. Add blue food coloring, a few drops at a time, to remaining icing to create sky blue; stir until evenly colored. Spread cookies with sky blue icing. Let stand 10 minutes or until set.

5. Pipe clouds using ¼ cup reserved white icing. Divide remaining ½ cup white icing into 2 small bowls. Add food coloring, a drop at a time, to each bowl to make dark blue and green icings. Pipe kites using dark blue and green icings. Pipe kite tails using yellow decorating icing. Let stand 10 minutes or until set.   *Makes about 1½ dozen cookies*

Royal Icing: Beat 4 cups powdered sugar, 6 tablespoons water and 3 tablespoons meringue powder in medium bowl with electric mixer at high speed until soft peaks form. Cover surface with plastic wrap until needed. Makes about 2 cups.

Snickerdoodle Batter Ups

1 package (about 16 ounces) refrigerated sugar cookie dough
1 teaspoon vanilla
¼ cup sugar
¼ teaspoon ground cinnamon
   Brown and red decorating icings

1. Let dough stand at room temperature 15 minutes.

2. Combine dough and vanilla in large bowl; beat with electric mixer at medium speed until well blended. Divide dough evenly into 2 discs. Wrap and refrigerate 1 hour.

3. Preheat oven to 350°F. For baseballs, roll out 1 disc dough between parchment paper to ¼-inch thickness. Cut out circles using 2½-inch round cookie cutter. Re-roll scraps, if necessary, to make a total of 12 circles. Place 2 inches apart on ungreased cookie sheet.

4. Combine sugar and cinnamon in small bowl. Sprinkle each cutout with ½ teaspoon cinnamon-sugar. Bake 8 minutes or until edges are lightly browned. Cool on cookie sheet 3 minutes. Remove to wire rack; cool completely.

5. For bats, roll out remaining 1 disc dough between parchment paper to ¼-inch thickness. Cut out 4-inch bat shapes using sharp knife. Re-roll scraps, if necessary, to make a total of 12 bats. Place 2 inches apart on ungreased cookie sheet.

6. Sprinkle each cutout with ½ teaspoon cinnamon-sugar. Bake 8 minutes or until edges are lightly browned. Cool on cookie sheet 3 minutes. Remove to wire rack; cool completely.

7. Pipe brown icing onto bat cookies to resemble tape on handles. Pipe red icing onto balls to resemble seams.

Makes 2 dozen cookies

Palm Trees

1 package (about 16 ounces) refrigerated break-apart sugar
    cookie dough (24 count)
1 container (16 ounces) white or vanilla frosting
    Green and brown gel food colorings
    Green sparkling sugar
    Assorted colored candy-coated sunflower seeds (optional)

1. Let dough stand at room temperature 5 minutes. Line cookie sheets with parchment paper.

2. Preheat oven to 325°F. Roll out dough between parchment paper to ¼-inch thickness. Cut out palm tree shapes with sharp knife (approximately 3×3-inch shapes). Place 2 inches apart on prepared cookie sheets. Refrigerate 15 minutes.

3. Bake 13 minutes or until set. Cool on cookie sheets 5 minutes. Remove to wire racks; cool completely.

4. Reserve half of frosting in small bowl. Add green food coloring, a few drops at a time, to remaining frosting; stir until evenly colored. Spread leafy part of cookies with green frosting. Sprinkle with sparkling sugar. Add sunflower seeds, if desired. Let stand 10 minutes or until set.

5. Add brown food coloring, a few drops at a time, to reserved frosting. Spread trunks of cookies with brown frosting. Use toothpick to create rough texture. Let stand 10 minutes or until set.   *Makes about 16 cookies*

Billiard Balls

3½ cups all-purpose flour
1 teaspoon salt
1½ cups sugar
1 cup (2 sticks) unsalted butter, softened
2 eggs
2 teaspoons vanilla
2 containers (16 ounces each) white or vanilla frosting
Assorted gel food colorings
Black decorating icing

1. Whisk flour and salt in medium bowl. Beat sugar and butter in large bowl with electric mixer at medium speed until light and fluffy. Add eggs, one at a time, beating until blended after each addition. Add vanilla; beat until blended. Gradually add flour mixture, beating until blended after each addition. Divide dough evenly into 2 discs. Wrap and refrigerate 1 hour.

2. Preheat oven to 350°F. Line cookie sheets with parchment paper. Working with 1 disc at a time, roll out dough between parchment paper to ⅜-inch thickness. Cut out 18 large circles with 3-inch round cookie cutter. Place 1 inch apart on prepared cookie sheets. Cut out 18 small circles with 1¼-inch round cookie cutter. Place 1 inch apart on separate prepared cookie sheet. Refrigerate 15 minutes.

3. Bake large circles 15 minutes or until set. Bake small circles 12 minutes or until set. Cool on cookie sheets 5 minutes. Remove to wire racks; cool completely.

4. Reserve one fourth of frosting. Divide remaining frosting evenly among small bowls and tint with food colorings to make desired colors. For "solids," spread large circles with tinted frosting. Let stand until set. For "stripes," spread center two thirds of each large circle with tinted frosting. Let stand until set. Spread remaining one third with reserved white frosting. Let stand until set.

5. Spread small circles with remaining white frosting. Pipe number in center with decorating icing. Spread thin layer of frosting on back of small circles and adhere to center of large circles. Let stand until set.

Makes 1½ dozen cookies

•Fun & Games•

Nothin' but Net

1 package (about 16 ounces) refrigerated sugar cookie dough
1¼ cups all-purpose flour
2 tablespoons powdered sugar
2 tablespoons lemon juice
Orange, white and black decorating icings

1. Let dough stand at room temperature 15 minutes.

2. Combine dough, flour, powdered sugar and lemon juice in large bowl; beat with electric mixer at medium speed until well blended. Divide dough evenly into 2 discs. Wrap and refrigerate at least 2 hours. Meanwhile, draw pattern for cookies on cardboard; cut out pattern.

3. Preheat oven to 350°F. Lightly grease cookie sheets. Working with 1 disc at a time, roll out dough between parchment paper to ¼-inch thickness. Cut out dough around pattern with sharp knife; remove pattern. Place 2 inches apart on prepared cookie sheets.

4. Bake 13 minutes or until edges are lightly browned. Cool on cookie sheets 2 minutes. Remove to wire racks; cool completely.

5. Decorate with icings as shown in photo.   *Makes 1½ dozen cookies*

Tip Creating your own cardboard patterns for cookie shapes is a cost-effective and creative way to make unique cookies for every occasion.

Tic-Tac-Toe Cookies

¾ cup (1½ sticks) butter, softened
¾ cup granulated sugar
1 large egg
1 teaspoon vanilla extract
2¼ cups all-purpose flour
½ teaspoon baking powder
¼ teaspoon salt
4 squares (1 ounce each) semi-sweet chocolate, melted
¼ cup powdered sugar
1 teaspoon water
½ cup "M&M's"® Chocolate Mini Baking Bits

In large bowl cream butter and granulated sugar until light and fluffy; beat in egg and vanilla. In small bowl combine flour, baking powder and salt; blend into creamed mixture. Reserve half of dough. Stir chocolate into remaining dough. Wrap and refrigerate doughs 30 minutes.

Working with one dough at a time on lightly floured surface, roll or pat into 7×4½-inch rectangle. Cut dough into 9 (7×½-inch) strips. Repeat with remaining dough. Place one strip chocolate dough on sheet of plastic wrap. Place one strip vanilla dough next to chocolate dough. Place second strip of chocolate dough next to vanilla dough to make bottom layer. Prepare second row by stacking strips on first row, alternating vanilla dough over chocolate, and chocolate dough over vanilla. Repeat with third row to complete 1 bar. Repeat entire process with remaining dough strips, starting with vanilla dough, to complete second bar. Wrap both bars and refrigerate 1 hour.

Preheat oven to 350°F. Lightly grease cookie sheets. Cut bars crosswise into ¼-inch slices. Place 2 inches apart on prepared cookie sheets. Bake 10 to 12 minutes. Cool on cookie sheets 2 minutes; cool completely on wire racks. In small bowl combine powdered sugar and water until smooth. Using icing to attach, decorate cookies with "M&M's"® Chocolate Mini Baking Bits to look like Tic-Tac-Toe games. Store in tightly covered container.

Makes 4 dozen cookies

Poker Night Cookies

3½ cups all-purpose flour
½ teaspoon salt
1½ cups sugar
1 cup (2 sticks) unsalted butter, softened
2 eggs
2 teaspoons vanilla
Red and black gel food colorings

1. Whisk flour and salt in medium bowl. Beat sugar and butter in large bowl with electric mixer at medium speed until light and fluffy. Add eggs, one at a time, beating until blended after each addition. Add vanilla; beat until blended.

2. Gradually add flour mixture, beating until blended after each addition. Divide dough in half; place in 2 separate medium bowls. Add red food coloring, a few drops at a time, to half of dough; beat until evenly colored. Add black food coloring, a few drops at a time, to remaining half of dough; beat until evenly colored. Shape each dough into disc; wrap and refrigerate 1 hour.

3. Preheat oven to 350°F. Line cookie sheets with parchment paper. Working with 1 disc at a time, roll out dough between parchment paper to ⅜-inch thickness. Cut out circles with 3-inch round cookie cutter. Place 1 inch apart on prepared cookie sheets. Cut out hearts, clubs, diamonds or spades from centers of circles using 1-inch card suite cookie cutters. Transfer red shapes to black circles and black shapes to red circles. Refrigerate 15 minutes.

4. Bake 15 minutes or until set. Cool on cookie sheets 5 minutes. Remove to wire racks; cool completely. *Makes 2 dozen cookies*

Silly Sunglasses

3½ cups all-purpose flour
½ teaspoon salt
1½ cups sugar
1 cup (2 sticks) unsalted butter, softened
2 eggs
2 teaspoons vanilla
24 to 32 fruit-flavored hard candies, crushed
Assorted colored decorating icings and decors

1. Whisk flour and salt in medium bowl. Beat sugar and butter in large bowl with electric mixer at medium speed until light and fluffy. Add eggs, one at a time, beating until blended after each addition. Add vanilla; beat until blended.

2. Gradually add flour mixture, beating until blended after each addition. Divide dough evenly into 2 discs. Wrap and refrigerate 1 hour.

3. Preheat oven to 350°F. Line cookie sheets with silicone mats or parchment paper. Working with 1 disc at a time, roll out dough between sheets of parchment paper to ¼-inch thickness. Cut out sunglasses shapes with sharp knife (approximately 4×2-inch shapes). Place 2 inches apart on prepared cookie sheets. Cut out lenses from sunglasses; discard. Refrigerate 15 minutes.

4. Sprinkle crushed candy into each lens opening. Bake 8 minutes or until candy is melted and cookies are set. Cool completely on cookie sheets. Decorate sunglasses with icings and decors as desired.

Makes about 1 dozen cookies

Favorite Foods

Tiny Hot Fudge Sundae Cups

1 package (about 16 ounces) refrigerated sugar cookie dough
⅓ cup unsweetened cocoa powder
5 to 7 cups vanilla ice cream
   Hot fudge ice cream topping
   Colored sprinkles
   Whipped cream
9 maraschino cherries, cut into quarters

1. Let dough stand at room temperature 15 minutes. Spray outsides of 36 mini (1¾-inch) muffin cups with nonstick cooking spray.

2. Preheat oven to 350°F. Combine dough and cocoa in large bowl; beat with electric mixer at medium speed until well blended. Divide dough into 36 equal pieces; shape each piece over outside of prepared muffin cup. Bake 10 minutes or until set. Cool on pans 10 minutes. Remove to wire racks; cool completely.

3. Fill each cookie cup with ice cream. Drizzle with hot fudge; top with sprinkles, whipped cream and cherry quarter. Serve immediately.

Makes 3 dozen sundae cups

Over Easy Cookies

1 package (about 16 ounces) refrigerated break-apart sugar
cookie dough (24 count)
1 package (14 ounces) white chocolate candy discs
Yellow gel food coloring
1 cup prepared white or vanilla frosting

1. Let dough stand at room temperature 5 minutes. Line cookie sheets with parchment paper.

2. Preheat oven to 325°F. Roll out dough between parchment paper to ¼-inch thickness. Cut out egg white shapes with sharp knife (approximately 3½×2½-inch shapes). Place egg whites 2 inches apart on prepared cookie sheets. Cut out yolks with 1¼-inch round cookie cutter. Place egg yolks 1 inch apart on separate prepared cookie sheet. Refrigerate 15 minutes.

3. Bake egg whites 15 minutes or until set. Bake egg yolks 10 minutes or until set. Cool on cookie sheets 5 minutes. Remove to wire racks; cool completely.

4. Microwave candy discs in medium microwavable bowl on HIGH 1 minute. Stir. Microwave at additional 15-second intervals until smooth and spreadable. Spread egg whites with candy mixture. Let stand on wire racks 10 minutes or until set.

5. Add food coloring, a few drops at a time, to frosting; stir until evenly colored. Spread egg yolks with yellow frosting. Spread thin layer of frosting on back of egg yolks and adhere to egg whites. Let stand 10 minutes or until set.

Makes about 1 dozen cookies

Makin' Bacon Cookies

1 package (about 16 ounces) refrigerated break-apart sugar
    cookie dough (24 count)
½ cup water, divided
    Red, brown and yellow gel food colorings

1. Let dough stand at room temperature 5 minutes. Line cookie sheets with parchment paper.

2. Preheat oven to 325°F. Roll out dough between parchment paper to ¼-inch thickness. Cut out bacon shapes with sharp knife (approximately 3½×1-inch shapes). Place 2 inches apart on prepared cookie sheets. Refrigerate 15 minutes.

3. Bake 13 minutes or until set. Cool on cookie sheets 5 minutes. Remove to wire racks; cool completely.

4. Place ¼ cup water in small bowl. Add a few drops of red and brown food colorings; stir until evenly colored. Place remaining ¼ cup water in another small bowl. Add a few drops of red and yellow food colorings; stir until evenly colored. Paint cookies to resemble bacon with small clean paintbrushes, using as little water as possible for color to saturate. Leave some areas unpainted to resemble bacon fat. Let stand 1 hour or until dry.

Makes about 2 dozen cookies

 **Tip** Do not use paintbrushes that have been used for anything but food. Inexpensive paintbrushes can be found in most drugstores and supermarkets in the school supplies aisle. You can mark the handle with colored electrical tape to make sure the right brushes stay in the kitchen.

Cupcake Cookies

3½ cups all-purpose flour
1 teaspoon salt
1½ cups sugar
1 cup (2 sticks) unsalted butter, softened
2 eggs
2 teaspoons vanilla
1½ containers (16 ounces each) white or vanilla frosting
Assorted gel food colorings
Large confetti sprinkles

1. Whisk flour and salt in medium bowl. Beat sugar and butter in large bowl with electric mixer at medium speed until light and fluffy. Add eggs, one at a time, beating until blended after each addition. Add vanilla; beat until blended.

2. Gradually add flour mixture, beating until blended after each addition. Divide dough evenly into 2 discs. Wrap and refrigerate 1 hour.

3. Preheat oven to 350°F. Line cookie sheets with parchment paper. Working with 1 disc at a time, roll out dough between parchment paper to ⅜-inch thickness. Cut out cupcake shapes with sharp knife (approximately 2½×2½-inch shapes). Place 1 inch apart on prepared cookie sheets. Refrigerate 15 minutes.

4. Bake 15 minutes or until set. Cool on cookie sheets 5 minutes. Remove to wire racks; cool completely.

5. Reserve half of frosting. Add food coloring, a few drops at a time, to remaining half of frosting; stir until evenly colored. Spread bottom half of cookies with frosting. Let stand 3 minutes or until just beginning to set. Press toothpick into frosting to create lines that resemble paper liner cups. Let stand on wire racks 10 minutes or until set.

6. Add food coloring, a few drops at a time, to reserved frosting; stir until evenly colored. (Divide frosting before adding food coloring if more colors are desired.) Spread top half of cookies with frosting. Press sprinkles into frosting. Let stand 10 minutes or until set.

Makes 2 dozen cookies

Watermelon Slices

2 packages (about 16 ounces each) refrigerated sugar cookie dough
½ cup all-purpose flour, divided
Green and red food colorings
Mini semisweet chocolate chips

1. Let doughs stand at room temperature 15 minutes.

2. Beat 1 package dough, ¼ cup flour and green food coloring in large bowl with electric mixer at medium speed until well blended. Shape into disc; wrap and refrigerate 2 hours.

3. Combine remaining package dough, remaining ¼ cup flour and red food coloring in separate large bowl; beat at medium speed until well blended. Shape into 9-inch-long log. Wrap and refrigerate 2 hours.

4. Roll out green dough between parchment paper into 9×8-inch rectangle. Place log in center of green rectangle. Fold edges up and around log; press edges to seal. Roll gently to form smooth log. Wrap and freeze 30 minutes.

5. Preheat oven to 350°F. Cut log into ⅜-inch-thick slices. Cut each slice in half. Place 2 inches apart on ungreased cookie sheets. Gently reshape, if necessary. Press several mini chocolate chips into each slice for watermelon seeds.

6. Bake 8 minutes or until set. Cool on cookie sheets 1 minute. Remove to wire racks; cool completely.

Makes about 4 dozen cookies

Burger Bliss

Buns

1 package (about 16 ounces) refrigerated sugar cookie dough
½ cup creamy peanut butter
⅓ cup all-purpose flour
¼ cup packed brown sugar
½ teaspoon vanilla
   Beaten egg white and sesame seeds (optional)

Burgers

½ (16-ounce) package refrigerated sugar cookie dough*
3 tablespoons unsweetened cocoa powder
2 tablespoons packed brown sugar
½ teaspoon vanilla
   Red, yellow and green decorating icings

Reserve remaining dough for another use.

1. Preheat oven to 350°F. Grease cookie sheets.

2. For buns, let 1 package dough stand at room temperature 15 minutes. Beat 1 package dough, peanut butter, flour, ¼ cup brown sugar and ½ teaspoon vanilla in large bowl with electric mixer at medium speed until blended. Shape into 48 (1-inch) balls; place 2 inches apart on prepared cookie sheets.

3. Bake 14 minutes or until lightly browned. Brush half of cookies with egg white and sprinkle with sesame seeds after 10 minutes, if desired. Cool on cookie sheets 2 minutes. Remove to wire racks; cool completely.

4. For burgers, let ½ package dough stand at room temperature 15 minutes. Beat dough, cocoa, 2 tablespoons brown sugar and ½ teaspoon vanilla in medium bowl at medium speed until blended. Shape into 24 (1-inch) balls; place 2 inches apart on prepared cookie sheets. Flatten to ¼-inch thickness.

5. Bake 12 minutes or until set. Cool on cookie sheets 2 minutes. Remove to wire racks; cool completely.

6. Use icing to attach burgers to flat sides of 24 buns. Pipe red, yellow and green icings on burgers. Top with remaining buns.

Makes 2 dozen sandwich cookies

Mighty Milkshakes

1 package (about 19 ounces) brownie mix, plus ingredients
   to prepare mix
1 package (14 ounces) milk chocolate or peanut butter
   candy discs
½ (16-ounce) container white or vanilla frosting
   Colored drinking straws
   Colored sprinkles

1. Preheat oven to 350°F. Coat 9-inch square baking pan with nonstick cooking spray.

2. Prepare brownie mix according to package directions; pour batter into prepared pan. Bake 35 minutes or until toothpick inserted into center comes out clean. Cool completely in pan on wire rack. Cover; freeze 1 hour or overnight.

3. Run knife around edges of brownies. Place cutting board over baking pan; invert and let stand until brownies release from pan. Trim edges; discard. Cut into 18 rectangles.

4. Microwave candy discs in medium microwavable bowl on HIGH 1 minute. Stir. Microwave at additional 15-second intervals until smooth and spreadable. Stand brownies up on small side. Spread all sides except bottom of brownies with candy mixture. Let stand on wire racks 10 minutes or until set.

5. Pipe frosting on top of each brownie for whipped cream. Decorate with straws and sprinkles.

Makes 1½ dozen brownies

Marshmallow Ice Cream Cone Cookies

1 package (about 16 ounces) refrigerated sugar cookie dough
6 ice cream sugar cones, broken into pieces
1 container (16 ounces) white frosting
1 package (about 10 ounces) colored miniature marshmallows
   Colored sprinkles

1. Let dough stand at room temperature 15 minutes.

2. Preheat oven to 350°F. Place sugar cones in food processor. Process using on/off pulsing action until finely ground. Combine dough and sugar cones in large bowl; beat until well blended.

3. Shape dough into 3 equal balls. Pat each ball into 9-inch circle on lightly floured surface. Cut each circle into 6 wedges; place 2 inches apart on ungreased cookie sheets.

4. Bake 10 minutes or until edges are lightly browned. While cookies are still warm, score crisscross pattern into cookies. Cool on cookie sheets 5 minutes. Remove cookies to wire racks; cool completely.

5. Spread 2-inch strip of frosting at wide end of each cookie. Press marshmallows into frosting; top with sprinkles.   *Makes 1½ dozen cookies*

Let's Celebrate

Birthday Cake Cookies

1 package (about 16 ounces) refrigerated sugar cookie dough
   Food coloring (optional)
1 container (16 ounces) white frosting
   Colored nonpareils or decors
10 small birthday candles

1. Preheat oven to 350°F. Lightly grease 10 mini (1¾-inch) muffin cups and 10 standard (2½-inch) muffin cups. Shape one third of dough into 10 (1-inch) balls; press into bottoms of prepared mini muffin cups. Shape remaining two thirds of dough into 10 equal balls; press into bottoms of prepared standard muffin cups.

2. Bake standard cookies 10 minutes or until edges are light brown. Bake mini cookies 8 minutes or until edges are light brown. Cool in pans 5 minutes. Remove to wire racks; cool completely.

3. Add food coloring, if desired, to frosting; mix well. Spread frosting over top and side of each cookie. Place 1 mini cookie on top of 1 standard cookie. Decorate with nonpareils. Press 1 candle into center of each cookie.

Makes 10 cookies

Earth Day Delights

3½ cups all-purpose flour
1 teaspoon salt
1½ cups sugar
1 cup (2 sticks) unsalted butter, softened
2 eggs
2 teaspoons vanilla
1½ cups chopped pecans
Royal Icing (recipe follows)
Blue and green gel food colorings

1. Whisk flour and salt in medium bowl. Beat sugar and butter in large bowl with electric mixer at medium speed until light and fluffy. Add eggs, one at a time, beating until blended after each addition. Add vanilla; beat until blended.

2. Gradually add flour mixture, beating until blended after each addition. Stir in pecans. Divide dough evenly into 2 discs. Wrap and refrigerate 1 hour.

3. Preheat oven to 350°F. Line cookie sheets with parchment paper. Working with 1 disc at a time, roll out dough between parchment paper to ⅜-inch thickness. Cut out circles with 3¼-inch round cookie cutter. Place 1 inch apart on prepared cookie sheets. Refrigerate 15 minutes.

4. Bake 15 minutes or until set. Cool on cookie sheets 5 minutes. Remove to wire racks; cool completely.

5. Prepare Royal Icing. Divide icing into 2 small bowls. Add blue food coloring to one bowl, a few drops at a time; stir until evenly colored. Spread cookies with blue icing. Let stand 10 minutes or until set.

6. Add green food coloring, a few drops at a time, to remaining bowl; stir until evenly colored. Pipe continent shapes using green icing. Let stand 10 minutes or until set. *Makes about 1½ dozen cookies*

Royal Icing: Beat 4 cups powdered sugar, 6 tablespoons water and 3 tablespoons meringue powder in medium bowl with electric mixer at high speed until soft peaks form. Cover surface with plastic wrap until needed. Makes about 2 cups.

Easter Nest Cookies

1½ cups all-purpose flour
1 teaspoon baking powder
½ teaspoon salt
¾ cup (1½ sticks) butter
2 cups miniature marshmallows
½ cup sugar
1 egg white
1 teaspoon vanilla extract
½ teaspoon almond extract
3¾ cups MOUNDS® Sweetened Coconut Flakes, divided
   JOLLY RANCHER® Jelly Beans
   HERSHEY'S Candy-Coated Milk Chocolate Eggs

1. Heat oven to 375°F.

2. Stir together flour, baking powder and salt; set aside. Place butter and marshmallows in microwave-safe bowl. Microwave at HIGH (100%) 1 to 1½ minutes or just until mixture melts when stirred. Beat sugar, egg white, vanilla and almond extract in separate bowl; add melted butter mixture, beating until light and fluffy. Gradually add flour mixture, beating until blended. Stir in 2 cups coconut.

3. Shape dough into 1-inch balls; roll balls in remaining 1¾ cups coconut, tinting coconut, if desired.* Place balls on ungreased cookie sheet. Press thumb into center of each ball, creating shallow depression.

4. Bake 8 to 10 minutes or just until lightly browned. Place 1 to 3 jelly beans and milk chocolate eggs in center of each cookie. Transfer to wire rack; cool completely. *Makes about 3½ dozen cookies*

To Tint Coconut: Place ¾ teaspoon water and a few drops food color in small bowl; stir in 1¾ cups coconut. Toss with fork until evenly tinted; cover tightly.

Liberty Bell Cookies

Cookies

    2 packages (about 17 ounces each) sugar cookie mix
    ¼ cup all-purpose flour
    ⅔ cup unsalted butter, melted
    2 eggs

Glaze

    ¼ cup powdered sugar
    1 teaspoon water
    ¼ teaspoon ground cinnamon
    ¼ teaspoon vanilla
    Brown decorating icing

1. Line cookie sheets with parchment paper. Combine cookie mix and flour in large bowl; stir well. Add butter and eggs; stir until well combined. Divide dough evenly into 2 discs. Wrap and refrigerate 1 hour.

2. Preheat oven to 375°F. Working with 1 disc at a time, roll out dough between parchment paper to ¼-inch thickness. Cut out shapes using 3-inch bell cookie cutter. Place 1 inch apart on prepared cookie sheets. Refrigerate 15 minutes.

3. Bake 10 minutes or until set. Cool on cookie sheets 5 minutes. Remove to wire racks; cool completely.

4. For glaze, combine powdered sugar, water, cinnamon and vanilla in small bowl; stir until smooth. Spread glaze over cookies. Let stand 15 minutes or until set. Outline bell and draw crack and clapper with decorating icing.

Makes 3 dozen cookies

Variation: You may used melted chocolate in place of the decorating icing. Place about 1 cup chocolate chips in resealable food storage bag. (Do not seal bag.) Microwave 30 seconds at a time until chocolate chips begin to soften and lose their shape. Remove from microwave, seal bag and knead until smooth. Snip off corner of bag and squeeze to outline bell and draw crack and clapper.

Window-to-My-Heart Cookies

2¼ cups all-purpose flour
½ teaspoon salt
¼ teaspoon baking powder
1 cup (2 sticks) butter, softened
½ cup powdered sugar
¼ cup packed brown sugar
1 teaspoon vanilla
1 cup dried cranberries, chopped
15 to 20 cherry- or cinnamon-flavored hard candies, crushed

1. Combine flour, salt and baking powder in medium bowl. Beat butter, powdered sugar, brown sugar and vanilla in large bowl with electric mixer at medium speed until creamy. Gradually add flour mixture, beating until blended after each addition. Stir in cranberries. Shape dough into disc; wrap and refrigerate 1 hour.

2. Preheat oven to 325°F. Line cookie sheets with silicone mats or parchment paper. Roll out dough between parchment paper to ¼-inch thickness. Cut out shapes using 2- to 3-inch heart cookie cutter. Cut out center of each cookie using smaller heart cookie cutter; re-roll scraps to make additional hearts.

3. Place 1 inch apart on prepared cookie sheets. Sprinkle crushed candy into each opening. Bake 20 minutes or until candy is melted and cookies are set. Cool completely on cookie sheets.

Makes about 3 dozen cookies

 Tip Silicone mats are available at home goods stores, specialty kitchen stores and online. Their reusability makes them a great option for environment-friendly baking when compared to single-use parchment paper.

Congrats Grad!

1 package (about 16 ounces) refrigerated sugar cookie dough
¼ cup all-purpose flour
¼ cup creamy peanut butter
1 cup mini semisweet chocolate chips
Granulated sugar
48 small gumdrops
Cookie Glaze (recipe follows)
Food coloring
12 graham cracker squares

1. Let dough stand at room temperature 15 minutes. Lightly grease 12 standard (2½-inch) muffin cups.

2. Preheat oven to 350°F. Combine dough, flour and peanut butter in large bowl; beat with electric mixer at medium speed until well blended. Stir in chocolate chips. Shape dough into 12 balls; press into bottoms of prepared muffin cups.

3. Bake 15 minutes or until lightly browned. Cool in pan 10 minutes. Remove to wire rack; cool completely.

4. Sprinkle sugar on waxed paper. For each tassel, slightly flatten 3 gumdrops. Place gumdrops, with ends overlapping slightly, on sugared surface. Roll flattened gumdrops into 3×1-inch piece, turning over frequently to coat with sugar. Trim and discard edges of gumdrop piece. Cut piece into 2½×¼-inch strips. Cut bottom part into several lengthwise strips to form fringe.

5. Prepare Cookie Glaze. Tint glaze with food coloring. Place cookies upside down on wire rack set over waxed paper. Spread glaze over cookies. Spread glaze over graham crackers; attach 1 cracker to top of each cookie. Place tassel on each cap. Set gumdrop on each tassel for cap button. Let stand 40 minutes or until set.

Makes 1 dozen cookies

Cookie Glaze: Combine 4 cups powdered sugar and 6 to 8 tablespoons milk, 1 tablespoon at a time, in medium bowl to make a pourable glaze. Makes about 2 cups.

Monogram Cookies

3½ cups all-purpose flour
1 teaspoon salt
1½ cups sugar
1 cup (2 sticks) unsalted butter, softened
2 eggs
2 teaspoons vanilla
Gel food coloring
1 container (16 ounces) white or vanilla frosting
Assorted jumbo nonpareils (optional)

1. Whisk flour and salt in medium bowl. Beat sugar and butter in large bowl with electric mixer at medium speed until light and fluffy. Add eggs, one at a time, beating until blended after each addition. Add vanilla; beat until blended.

2. Gradually add flour mixture, beating until blended after each addition. Divide dough evenly into 2 discs. Wrap and refrigerate 1 hour.

3. Preheat oven to 350°F. Line cookie sheets with parchment paper.

4. Working with 1 disc at a time, roll out dough between parchment paper to ⅜-inch thickness. Cut out circles with 3-inch fluted round cookie cutter. Place 1 inch apart on prepared cookie sheets. Cut out letters using 1-inch alphabet cookie cutters; discard. Refrigerate 15 minutes.

5. Bake 15 minutes or until set. Cool on cookie sheets 5 minutes. Remove to wire racks; cool completely.

6. Add food coloring, a few drops at a time, to frosting; stir until evenly colored. Spread cookies with frosting. Decorate with nonpareils as desired. Let stand 10 minutes or until set.

Makes 2 dozen cookies

Hanukkah Coin Cookies

1 cup (2 sticks) butter or margarine, softened
1 cup sugar
1 egg
1 teaspoon vanilla extract
1¾ cups all-purpose flour
½ cup HERSHEY'S Cocoa
1½ teaspoons baking powder
½ teaspoon salt
Buttercream Frosting (recipe follows)

1. Beat butter, sugar, egg and vanilla in large bowl until well blended. Stir together flour, cocoa, baking powder and salt; gradually add to butter mixture, beating until well blended. Divide dough in half; place each half on separate sheet of wax paper.

2. Shape each portion into log, about 7 inches long. Wrap each log in wax paper or plastic wrap. Refrigerate until firm, at least 8 hours.

3. Heat oven to 325°F. Cut logs into ¼-inch-thick slices. Place on ungreased cookie sheet.

4. Bake 8 to 10 minutes or until set. Cool slightly; remove from cookie sheet to wire rack. Cool completely. Prepare Buttercream Frosting; spread over tops of cookies.   *Makes about 4½ dozen cookies*

Buttercream Frosting

¼ cup (½ stick) butter, softened
1½ cups powdered sugar
1 to 2 tablespoons milk
½ teaspoon vanilla extract
Yellow food color

Beat butter in large bowl until creamy. Gradually add powdered sugar and milk to butter, beating to desired consistency. Stir in vanilla and food color.

Makes about 1 cup

Cookie Creations

Lollipop Flower Pots

1 package (about 16 ounces) refrigerated sugar cookie dough
36 caramels
1 cup chocolate cookie crumbs
Green gummy fruit slices or candy spearmint leaves
36 small lollipops

1. Let dough stand at room temperate 15 minutes. Preheat oven to 350°F. Lightly grease 36 mini (1¾-inch) muffin cups.

2. Shape dough into 36 balls; press onto bottoms and up sides of prepared muffin cups. Place 1 caramel in center of each muffin cup.

3. Bake 10 minutes or until edges are lightly browned. Cool in pans 2 minutes. Remove to wire racks; cool completely.

4. Sprinkle cookie crumbs evenly into center of cookies. Flatten gummy fruit slices slightly; press into leaf shapes. Push 1 lollipop and 2 leaves into each cookie.   *Makes 3 dozen cookies*

Marshmallow Chipper Cookie Cake

3½ cups all-purpose flour
1 teaspoon *each* baking powder, baking soda and salt
1 cup packed light brown sugar
½ cup granulated sugar
3 cups (6 sticks) unsalted butter, softened, divided
2 eggs
2 egg yolks
2 teaspoons vanilla, divided
2 cups (12 ounces) semisweet chocolate chips
2 cups powdered sugar
2 containers (7 ounces each) marshmallow creme

1. Whisk flour, baking powder, baking soda and salt in medium bowl. Combine brown sugar and granulated sugar in large bowl. Add 1 cup butter; beat with electric mixer at medium speed until light and fluffy. Add eggs, one at a time, beating until blended after each addition. Add egg yolks and 1 teaspoon vanilla; beat until blended.

2. Gradually add flour mixture, beating until blended after each addition. Stir in chocolate chips. Divide dough evenly into 3 discs. Wrap and refrigerate overnight.

3. Preheat oven to 325°F. Line cookie sheets with parchment paper. Working with 1 disc at a time, roll out dough between parchment paper into 8-inch circle about ½ inch thick. Transfer to prepared cookie sheets; refrigerate 15 minutes. Bake 25 minutes or until light brown and set. Cool on cookie sheets 5 minutes. Remove to wire racks; cool completely.

4. Beat remaining 2 cups butter in another large bowl at medium speed until smooth. Gradually add powdered sugar, beating until blended after each addition. Beat at high speed 2 minutes or until light and fluffy. Add remaining 1 teaspoon vanilla; beat until blended. Stir in marshmallow creme.

5. Place 1 cookie on serving plate. Spread with half of marshmallow mixture. Repeat layers. Top with remaining cookie. Cover; refrigerate 1 hour before slicing. *Makes 16 to 20 servings*

Chocolate Swirl Lollipop Cookies

½ cup (1 stick) butter or margarine, softened
1 cup sugar
2 eggs
1 teaspoon orange extract
1 teaspoon vanilla extract
2¼ cups all-purpose flour, divided
½ teaspoon baking soda
½ teaspoon salt
¼ teaspoon freshly grated orange peel
Few drops red and yellow food color (optional)
2 sections (½ ounce each) HERSHEY®S Unsweetened Chocolate
     Baking Bar, melted
About 24 wooden popsicle sticks

1. Beat butter and sugar in large bowl until blended. Add eggs and extracts; beat until light and fluffy. Gradually add 1¼ cups flour, blending until smooth. Stir in remaining 1 cup flour, baking soda and salt until mixture is well blended.

2. Place half of batter in medium bowl; stir in orange peel. Stir in food color, if desired. Melt chocolate as directed on package; stir into remaining half of batter. Cover; refrigerate both mixtures until firm enough to roll.

3. With rolling pin or fingers, between 2 pieces of wax paper, roll chocolate and orange mixtures each into 10×8-inch rectangle. Remove wax paper; place orange mixture on top of chocolate. Starting on longest side, roll up doughs tightly, forming into 12-inch roll; wrap in plastic wrap. Refrigerate until firm.

4. Heat oven to 350°F. Remove plastic wrap from roll; cut into ½-inch-wide slices. Place on cookie sheet at least 3 inches apart. Insert popsicle stick into each cookie.

5. Bake 8 to 10 minutes or until cookie is almost set. Cool slightly; remove from cookie sheet to wire rack. Cool completely. Decorate and tie with ribbon, if desired.

Makes about 2 dozen cookies

•Cookie Creations•

Christmas Cookie Tree

2 packages (about 16 ounces each) refrigerated sugar cookie dough
2 to 3 tubes (about 4 ounces each) green decorating icing with tips
1 tube (about 4 ounces) yellow decorating icing
1 tube (about 4 ounces) red decorating icing

1. Let dough stand at room temperature 5 minutes. Preheat oven to 350°F. Line cookie sheets with parchment paper.

2. Roll out 1 package dough between parchment paper to ¼-inch thickness. Cut out 7-inch circle* and 6½-inch circle using sharp knife. Transfer circles to prepared cookie sheet. Reserve scraps; wrap and refrigerate.

3. Repeat step 2 with remaining package dough, cutting out 6-inch circle and 5½-inch circle. Transfer to prepared cookie sheet. Bake 10 minutes or until edges are lightly browned. Cool on cookie sheets 2 minutes. Remove parchment paper to wire racks; cool completely before removing cookies from parchment paper.

4. Repeat step 3 using scraps to make 8 more circles, each ½ inch smaller in diameter. Reduce baking time as circles get smaller.

5. To assemble tree, secure largest cookie to serving platter with icing. Using leaf tip and green icing, pipe leaves around outer edge of cookie. Place small amount of icing in center of cookie. Add next largest cookie and repeat layers, adding cookies largest to smallest.

6. Pipe garlands around tree using yellow icing. Pipe ornaments using red icing. Serve cookies individually by separating layers or cutting into pieces with serrated knife.

Makes 12 to 15 servings

Use a compass to draw 12 circles, each one ½ inch smaller, on parchment paper; cut out and use as patterns to cut dough circles. For a free-form look, use various bowls, glasses and biscuit cutters to trace and cut out 12 graduated circles.

Freaky Fruity Fish Bowl Cookie

1 package (about 16 ounces) refrigerated sugar cookie dough
2 packages (8 ounces each) cream cheese, softened
⅓ cup milk
⅔ cup powdered sugar
½ teaspoon vanilla
   Blue food coloring
   Blueberries, rinsed and patted dry
   Canned mandarin oranges, well drained and patted dry
   Green seedless grapes, sliced lengthwise, patted dry
   Gummy fish candies
   Sea creature fruit snacks
   Assorted colored decorating sugars

1. Let dough stand at room temperature 5 minutes. Preheat oven to 350°F. Spray cookie sheet with nonstick cooking spray.

2. Reserve one fourth of dough; set aside. Place remaining dough on prepared cookie sheet; flatten into 11×9-inch oval. Shape reserved dough into 2×12-inch strip and place on top of oval to make fish bowl shape.

3. Bake 13 minutes or until lightly golden. Cool completely on cookie sheet on wire rack.

4. Beat cream cheese and milk in medium bowl with electric mixer at medium speed until blended. Add powdered sugar and vanilla; beat at low speed until smooth. Reserve ⅓ cup frosting in small bowl. Add food coloring, a few drops at a time, to remaining frosting; beat until evenly colored.

5. Spread blue frosting over "bowl" area and reserved white frosting over "rim" area of cookie. Decorate with fruit, gummy candies, fruit snacks and decorating sugars as desired. *Makes 16 servings*

Whirligigs

1 package (about 16 ounces) refrigerated sugar cookie dough
¼ cup all-purpose flour
½ teaspoon each banana and strawberry extract (optional)
   Yellow and red food colorings
   Colored sugar (optional)
12 (8-inch) lollipop sticks or wooden popsicle sticks*

Lollipop sticks and popsicle sticks are available at craft stores and where cake decorating supplies are sold.

1. Let dough stand at room temperature 15 minutes. Grease cookie sheets.

2. Combine dough and flour; beat with electric mixer at medium speed until well blended. Divide dough in half; place in separate medium bowls. Add banana extract, if desired, and yellow food coloring to one bowl. Add strawberry extract, if desired, and red food coloring to remaining bowl. Beat doughs separately at medium speed until well blended. Shape each dough into disc; wrap and freeze 30 minutes.

3. Preheat oven to 350°F. Shape red dough into rope about 18 inches long on lightly floured surface. Repeat with yellow dough. Twist ropes together. Divide rope into 3 equal pieces. Working with 1 piece at a time, shape dough into rope about 20 inches long. Cut into 4 equal pieces. Coil each piece into circle; place 2 inches apart on prepared cookie sheets. (Make sure to leave room for lollipop sticks.) Sprinkle cookies with colored sugar, if desired. Refrigerate 15 minutes.

4. Carefully press lollipop stick into edge of each cookie. Bake 12 minutes or until set. Cool completely on cookie sheets on wire racks.

Makes 1 dozen cookies

Snapshot Cookies

3½ cups all-purpose flour
1 teaspoon salt
1½ cups sugar
1 cup (2 sticks) unsalted butter, softened
2 eggs
2 teaspoons vanilla
Royal Icing (recipe follows)
Black gel food coloring
Assorted colored round candies
12 mini gummy candies

1. Whisk flour and salt in medium bowl. Beat sugar and butter in large bowl with electric mixer at medium speed until light and fluffy. Add eggs, one at a time, beating until blended after each addition. Add vanilla; beat until blended. Gradually add flour mixture, beating until blended after each addition. Divide dough evenly into 2 discs. Wrap and refrigerate 1 hour or until chilled.

2. Preheat oven to 350°F. Line cookie sheets with parchment paper. Working with 1 disc at a time, roll out dough between parchment paper to ⅜-inch thickness. From each disc, cut out 6 rectangles with sharp knife (approximately 2½×3½-inch shapes) and 6 circles with 1½-inch round cookie cutter.

3. Place rectangles 2 inches apart on prepared cookie sheets. Place circles 1 inch apart on separate prepared cookie sheet. Refrigerate 15 minutes. Bake rectangles 15 minutes or until set. Bake circles 12 minutes or until set. Cool on cookie sheets 5 minutes. Remove to wire racks; cool completely.

4. Prepare Royal Icing; reserve 1 cup. Add food coloring, a few drops at a time, to remaining icing; stir until evenly colored. Spread rectangles with black icing. Spread circles with reserved white icing. Spread white icing on back of circles and adhere to rectangles for lens. Dot back of candies with icing and adhere for flash, viewfinder and lens. Dot back of gummy candy with icing and adhere to side of rectangle for button. Let stand until set.   *Makes 1 dozen cookies*

Royal Icing: Beat 4 cups powdered sugar, 6 tablespoons water and 3 tablespoons meringue powder in medium bowl with electric mixer at high speed until soft peaks form. Cover surface with plastic wrap until needed. Makes about 2 cups.

Surprise Cookies

2 squares (1 ounce each) semisweet baking chocolate, coarsely chopped
1¼ cups all-purpose flour
½ teaspoon baking powder
¼ teaspoon salt
½ cup (1 stick) butter, softened
½ cup sugar
1 egg
1 teaspoon vanilla
Fillings: well-drained maraschino cherries or candied cherries; chocolate mint candies, broken into halves; white chocolate baking bar, cut into chunks; milk chocolate candy bar, cut into chunks; semisweet chocolate chunks; raspberry jam; or apricot preserves
Sprinkles or nonpareils (optional)

1. Preheat oven to 350°F. Lightly grease 12 mini (1¾-inch) muffin cups.

2. Melt chocolate in small heavy saucepan over low heat, stirring constantly; remove from heat. Combine flour, baking powder and salt in small bowl.

3. Beat butter and sugar in large bowl with electric mixer at medium speed 2 minutes or until light and fluffy. Beat in egg and vanilla. Beat in melted chocolate. Gradually add flour mixture, beating at low speed until blended after each addition.

4. Drop dough by level teaspoonfuls into prepared muffin cups. Form small indentation in center of batter.

5. Fill as desired with assorted fillings. Top with heaping teaspoonful of dough, smoothing top lightly. Top with sprinkles, if desired.

6. Bake 15 minutes or until set. Cool completely in pan on wire rack.

Makes 1 dozen cookies

Tip: Store these cookies tightly covered at room temperature. They do not freeze well.

Contents

Reinvented Classics 194

Game's On! 212

Quirky Bites 228

Kiddie Creations...........................246

Sweet Surprises.............................. 262

Acknowledgments...........................280

Index 281

Reinvented Classics

Micro Mini Stuffed Potatoes

1 pound small new red potatoes
¼ cup sour cream
2 tablespoons butter, softened
½ teaspoon minced garlic
¼ cup milk
½ cup (2 ounces) shredded sharp Cheddar cheese
½ teaspoon salt
¼ teaspoon black pepper
¼ cup finely chopped green onions (optional)

Microwave Directions

1. Pierce potatoes with fork in several places. Microwave potatoes on HIGH 5 to 6 minutes or until fork-tender. Let stand 5 minutes; cut in half lengthwise. Scoop out pulp from potatoes; set potato shells aside.

2. Beat potato pulp in medium bowl with electric mixer at low speed 30 seconds. Add sour cream, butter and garlic; beat until well blended. Gradually add milk, beating until smooth. Add cheese, salt and pepper; beat until blended.

3. Fill each potato shell with equal amounts of potato mixture. Microwave on HIGH 1 to 2 minutes or until cheese is melted. Garnish with green onions.

Makes 4 servings

Grilled Cheese Kabobs

8 thick slices whole wheat bread
3 thick slices sharp Cheddar cheese
3 thick slices Monterey Jack or Colby Jack cheese
2 tablespoons butter, melted

1. Cut each bread slice into 1-inch squares. Cut each cheese slice into 1-inch squares. Make small sandwiches with one square of bread and one square of each type of cheese. Top with second square of bread.

2. Place sandwiches on ends of short wooden skewers. Brush sides of sandwiches with melted butter.

3. Heat nonstick grill pan over medium-high heat. Grill sandwich kabobs 30 seconds on each side or until golden brown and cheese is melted.

Makes 12 servings

Hawaiian Pizza Bites

1 canister (13.9 ounces) refrigerated pizza crust dough
¾ cup pizza sauce
1½ cups (6 ounces) shredded mozzarella cheese
3 ounce sliced Canadian bacon, cut into small pieces
1 can (8 ounces) DOLE® Pineapple Tidbits *or* 1 can (20 ounce)
   DOLE® Pineapple Chunks, drained

• Unroll dough onto lightly floured surface. Cut 15 to 16 circles with 3-inch cookie or biscuit cutter and place them on cookie sheet sprayed with nonstick vegetable cooking spray.

• Bake at 400°F. 8 minutes. Remove from oven. Top crusts with pizza sauce, one-half cheese, Canadian bacon and pineapple tidbits. Top with remaining cheese.

• Bake an additional 6 to 10 minutes or until crusts are golden brown.

Makes 15 to 16 pizza bites

Prep Time: 10 minutes
Bake Time: 14 to 18 minutes

Meat Loaf Cupcakes

3 medium potatoes, peeled and chopped
1½ pounds ground beef
½ cup finely chopped onion
⅓ cup old-fashioned oats
1 egg
2 tablespoons chopped fresh rosemary leaves
½ cup milk
2 tablespoons butter
1 teaspoon salt
Black pepper
¼ cup snipped fresh chives

1. Preheat oven to 350°F. Place potatoes in medium saucepan; cover with water. Bring to a boil; cook 25 minutes or until potatoes are fork-tender.

2. Meanwhile, combine beef, onion, oats, egg and rosemary in large bowl; mix well. Divide mixture among 10 standard (2½-inch) muffin cups or silicone liners. Bake 25 minutes or until cooked through (160°F).

3. Beat potatoes, milk, butter, salt and pepper in large bowl with electric mixer at medium speed 3 minutes or until smooth. Place mashed potato mixture in large piping bag fitted with large star tip.

4. Remove meat loaf cupcakes to serving platter. Pipe mashed potatoes on top. Sprinkle with chives.

Makes 10 servings

Mac and Cheese Mini Cups

3 tablespoons butter, divided
2 tablespoons all-purpose flour
1 cup milk
1 teaspoon salt
½ teaspoon black pepper
1 cup (4 ounces) shredded sharp Cheddar cheese
1 cup (4 ounces) shredded Muenster cheese
½ pound elbow macaroni, cooked and drained
⅓ cup plain dry bread crumbs

1. Preheat oven to 400°F. Melt 1 tablespoon butter in large saucepan over medium heat. Grease 36 mini (1¾-inch) muffin cups with melted butter.

2. Melt remaining 2 tablespoons butter in same saucepan over medium heat. Whisk in flour; cook and stir 2 minutes. Add milk, salt and pepper; cook and stir 3 minutes or until mixture is thickened.

3. Remove from heat; stir in cheeses. Fold in macaroni. Divide mixture among prepared muffin cup. Sprinkle with bread crumbs.

4. Bake 20 minutes or until golden brown. Cool in pans 10 minutes. Remove carefully using sharp knife.   *Makes 36 appetizers*

 Tip Make this appetizer more fun by adding your favorite mix-ins like green peas, bacon bits or chopped tomatoes.

Mini Dizzy Dogs

½ sheet refrigerated crescent roll dough (half of 8-ounce can)
20 mini hot dogs or smoked sausages
   Ketchup and mustard

1. Preheat oven to 375°F. Line baking sheet with parchment paper.

2. Cut dough lengthwise into 20 (¼-inch) strips. Wrap 1 dough strip around entire length of 1 hot dog. Place on prepared baking sheet. Repeat with remaining dough strips and hot dogs.

3. Bake 10 minutes or until light golden brown. Serve with ketchup and mustard for dipping.   *Makes 20 appetizers*

Italian Chicken Nuggets

¼ cup all-purpose flour
 1 egg, lightly beaten
 1 cup plain dry bread crumbs
½ cup grated Parmesan cheese
 2 teaspoons Italian seasoning
   Salt and black pepper
 3 boneless skinless chicken breasts, cut into 1-inch pieces
   Warm pasta sauce

1. Preheat oven to 400°F. Line baking sheet with parchment paper.

2. Place flour in shallow bowl. Place egg in second shallow bowl. Combine bread crumbs, cheese, Italian seasoning, salt and pepper in third shallow bowl.

3. Dip each piece of chicken into flour, then in egg, then in bread crumb mixture. Place on prepared baking sheet.

4. Bake 25 minutes or until browned. Serve with warm pasta sauce for dipping.   *Makes 4 servings*

BLT Biscuits

2 cups all-purpose flour

2 teaspoons sugar

2 teaspoons baking powder

1 teaspoon black pepper

½ teaspoon baking soda

½ teaspoon salt

⅓ cup cold butter, cut into small pieces

1 cup (4 ounces) shredded Cheddar cheese

¾ cup buttermilk

½ cup mayonnaise

1 package (16 ounces) bacon slices, crisp-cooked and cut crosswise into 3 pieces

1 small head romaine lettuce, torn into small pieces

4 plum tomatoes, cut into ¼-inch slices

1. Preheat oven to 425°F. Line baking sheets with parchment paper.

2. Combine flour, sugar, baking powder, pepper, baking soda and salt in large bowl. Cut in butter with pastry blender or two knives until mixture resembles coarse crumbs. Stir in cheese and buttermilk just until mixture forms dough.

3. Turn dough out onto lightly floured surface; knead gently several times. Pat into 8×6-inch rectangle (about ¾ inch thick). Cut dough into 24 squares with sharp knife; place on prepared baking sheets.

4. Bake 10 to 12 minutes or until golden brown. Cool slightly on wire rack.

5. Split biscuits; spread each half with mayonnaise. Layer each biscuit with bacon, lettuce and tomato. *Makes 24 mini sandwiches*

Turkey Club Biscuits: Prepare BLT Biscuits as directed above, adding deli sliced turkey and avocado slices.

Sloppy Joe Sliders

12 ounces ground beef
 1 can (about 14 ounces) stewed tomatoes with Mexican seasonings, undrained
½ cup frozen mixed vegetables, thawed
½ cup chopped green bell pepper
 3 tablespoons ketchup
 2 teaspoons Worcestershire sauce
 1 teaspoon ground cumin
 1 teaspoon cider vinegar
24 mini whole wheat rolls or 1-ounce rolls, split and warmed

1. Brown beef 6 to 8 minutes in large nonstick skillet over medium-high heat, stirring to break up meat. Drain fat.

2. Add tomatoes, mixed vegetables, bell pepper, ketchup, Worcestershire sauce, cumin and vinegar; bring to a boil. Reduce heat; cover and simmer 15 minutes or until peppers are tender and mixture is thickened.

3. To serve, spoon 2 tablespoons beef mixture on each bun.

Makes 24 mini sandwiches

Tuna Schooners

  1 can (6 ounces) tuna packed in water, drained and flaked
½ cup finely chopped apple
¼ cup shredded carrot
⅓ cup ranch dressing
  2 English muffins, split and lightly toasted
  8 triangular-shaped tortilla chips

1. Combine tuna, apple and carrot in medium bowl. Add dressing; mix well.

2. Evenly spread tuna mixture on top of each muffin half. Press 2 chips firmly into tuna mixture for sails.

Makes 4 servings

 *Tip* This fun snack can be made using your favorite tuna salad recipe. For a sweet flavor and extra color, add some chopped red or green grapes.

Croque Monsieur Bites

8 thin slices firm sandwich bread
4 slices Swiss cheese, cut in half (about 4 ounces)
4 slices smoked ham (about 4 ounces)
   Dash grated nutmeg
2 tablespoons butter, melted

1. Cut crusts from bread slices; discard crusts. Place 4 slices of bread on work surface. Layer each with half slice of cheese, 1 slice of ham and remaining half slice of cheese; sprinkle with nutmeg. Top with remaining 4 slices of bread. Brush outsides of sandwiches with melted butter.

2. Heat large skillet over medium heat; cook sandwiches 2 minutes per side or until golden brown and cheese is melted. To serve, cut into quarters.

Makes 16 pieces

 **Tip** These sandwiches can be prepared ahead of time and reheated for an easy party appetizer. Leave sandwiches whole after cooking and refrigerate until ready to serve. Cut into quarters and place on foil-lined baking sheet. Bake in preheated 350°F oven 8 minutes or until sandwiches are heated through and cheese is melted.

Game's On!

Tiny Shrimp Tacos with Peach Salsa

1 peach, peeled and finely diced
2 tablespoons finely chopped red onion
1 jalapeño pepper,* finely chopped
  Juice of 1 lime
1 tablespoon chopped fresh cilantro or Italian parsley
1 clove garlic, minced
½ teaspoon salt
8 (6-inch) flour tortillas
1 tablespoon vegetable oil
1 pound medium raw shrimp, peeled, deveined and chopped
2 teaspoons chili powder

Jalapeño peppers can sting and irritate the skin, so wear rubber gloves when handling peppers and do not touch your eyes.

1. Combine peach, onion, jalapeño, lime juice, cilantro, garlic and salt in medium glass bowl. Set aside.

2. Preheat oven to 400°F. Cut out 24 rounds from tortillas with 2½-inch biscuit cutter or sharp knife. Discard scraps. Fold tortilla rounds over handle of wooden spoon; secure with toothpicks. Place on baking sheet. Repeat with remaining tortilla rounds. Bake 5 minutes.

3. Heat oil in large nonstick skillet over medium-high heat. Add shrimp and chili powder; cook and stir 3 minutes or until shrimp are pink and opaque.

4. Serve shrimp in taco shells with peach salsa.   *Makes 24 tacos*

Buffalo Wedges

3 pounds unpeeled Yukon Gold potatoes
3 tablespoons hot pepper sauce
2 tablespoons butter, melted
2 teaspoons smoked or sweet paprika
   Blue cheese dressing

1. Preheat oven to 400°F. Spray baking sheet with nonstick cooking spray. Cut each potato into 4 to 6 wedges, depending on size of potato.

2. Combine hot pepper sauce, butter and paprika in large bowl. Add potato wedges; toss to coat. Place wedges in single layer on prepared baking sheet.

3. Bake 20 minutes. Turn potatoes; bake 20 minutes or until light golden brown and crisp. Serve with blue cheese dressing for dipping.

Makes 4 servings

Hot Cheesy Chili Dip

1 pound ground beef
½ cup chopped onion
1 package (1 pound) pasteurized process cheese product with
   jalapeño pepper, cut into cubes
1 can (15 ounces) kidney beans, drained
1 bottle (12 ounces) HEINZ® Chili Sauce
¼ cup chopped fresh parsley
   Tortilla chips or crackers

In large saucepan, cook beef and onion until onion is tender; drain. Stir in cheese, beans and chili sauce; heat, stirring until cheese is melted. Stir in parsley. Serve warm with tortilla chips or crackers.   *Makes about 5 cups*

Beer-Braised Meatballs

  1 pound ground beef
½ cup Italian dry bread crumbs
½ cup grated Parmesan cheese
  2 eggs, lightly beaten
⅓ cup finely chopped onion
  2 cloves garlic, minced
½ teaspoon black pepper
¼ teaspoon salt
  1 bottle (12 ounces) light-colored beer, such as lager
1½ cups tomato sauce
  1 cup ketchup
½ cup packed brown sugar
  2 tablespoons tomato paste

1. Preheat oven to 400°F. Line broiler pan with foil; spray rack with nonstick cooking spray.

2. Combine beef, bread crumbs, cheese, eggs, onion, garlic, pepper and salt in large bowl; shape mixture into 1-inch balls.

3. Place meatballs on broiler rack. Bake 10 minutes or until browned.

4. Combine beer, tomato sauce, ketchup, brown sugar and tomato paste in Dutch oven. Bring to a boil. Add meatballs and reduce heat. Cover and simmer 20 to 30 minutes or until meatballs are cooked through (160°F), stirring occasionally.

Makes 20 meatballs

Pizza Fries

1 bag (2 pounds) frozen French fries
1 cup PREGO® Traditional or any variety PREGO® Italian Sauce
1½ cups shredded mozzarella cheese (about 6 ounces)
  Diced pepperoni (optional)

1. Prepare the fries according to the package directions. Remove them from the oven. Pour the Italian sauce over the fries.

2. Top with the cheese and pepperoni, if desired.

3. Bake for 5 minutes or until the cheese is melted.   *Makes 8 servings*

Prep Time: 20 minutes
Bake Time: 5 minutes

Poblano Pepper Kabobs

1 large poblano pepper*
4 ounces smoked turkey breast, cut into 8 cubes
4 ounces pepper jack cheese, cut into 8 cubes
¼ cup salsa (optional)

Poblano peppers can sting and irritate the skin, so wear rubber gloves when handling peppers and do not touch your eyes.

1. Preheat oven to 400°F. Fill medium saucepan half full with water; bring to a boil over medium-high heat. Add pepper; cook 1 minute. Drain. Core, seed and cut pepper into 12 bite-size pieces.

2. Thread 1 piece pepper, 1 piece turkey and 1 piece cheese onto each skewer. Repeat, ending with pepper. Place kabobs on baking sheet.

3. Bake 3 minutes or until cheese just begins to melt. Serve with salsa, if desired.   *Makes 4 servings*

Guacamole Sliders

    1 ripe avocado
    1 tablespoon ORTEGA® Fire-Roasted Diced Green Chiles
    1 tablespoon chopped cilantro
    1 tablespoon lime juice
  ⅛ teaspoon salt
    1 pound lean ground beef
    1 tablespoon water
    1 cup ORTEGA® Garden Vegetable Salsa, Medium, divided
  12 dinner rolls

CUT avocado in half and remove pit. Scoop out avocado with spoon and place in small bowl. Add chiles, cilantro, lime juice and salt. Gently mash with fork until blended; set aside.

COMBINE beef, water and ½ cup salsa in medium bowl. Form mixture into 12 small round balls. Flatten slightly.

GRILL or pan-fry burgers about 3 minutes. Turn over and flatten with spatula. Cook 4 minutes longer or until desired doneness.

CUT each roll in half. Fill with 1 tablespoon remaining salsa, 1 burger and 1 heaping tablespoon guacamole. Serve immediately.

Makes 12 small burgers

Note: Try using a panini press or similar double-sided grill to cook the sliders even faster.

Prep Time: 10 minutes
Start-to-Finish Time: 20 minutes

Baked Pork Buns

1 tablespoon vegetable oil
2 cups coarsely chopped bok choy
1 small onion *or* large shallot, thinly sliced
1 container (18 ounces) refrigerated shredded barbecue pork
   All-purpose flour
2 packages (10 ounces each) refrigerated buttermilk biscuit dough
   (5 count each)

1. Preheat oven to 350°F. Grease baking sheets.

2. Heat oil in large skillet over medium-high heat. Add bok choy and onion; cook and stir 8 minutes or until vegetables are tender. Remove from heat; stir in barbecue pork.

3. Lightly dust work surface with flour. Separate biscuit dough into individual biscuits. Split each biscuit in half crosswise to create two thin biscuits. Roll each biscuit half into 5-inch circle.

4. Spoon heaping tablespoon pork mixture onto one side of each circle. Fold dough over filling to form half circle; press edges to seal. Arrange buns on prepared baking sheets.

5. Bake 12 minutes or until golden brown.

Makes 20 buns

Chili Cheese Mini Dogs

    2 teaspoons chili powder
    ½ sheet refrigerated crescent roll dough (half of 8-ounce can)
    5 slices sharp Cheddar cheese
   20 mini hot dogs

1. Preheat oven to 375°F. Line baking sheet with parchment paper.

2. Sprinkle 1 teaspoon chili powder evenly over each side of dough. Cut dough into 20 squares.

3. Cut each cheese slice into 4 squares. Press 1 cheese square onto 1 dough square. Place 1 hot dog in center; bring up sides of dough to secure hot dog. Place on prepared baking sheet. Repeat with remaining cheese, dough and hot dogs.

4. Bake 12 minutes or until golden brown.   *Makes 20 servings*

Mini Reuben Skewers with Dipping Sauce

    ⅓ cup HELLMANN'S® or BEST FOODS® Real Mayonnaise
    ⅓ cup WISH-BONE® Thousand Island Dressing
     1 can (8 ounces) sauerkraut, drained and coarsely chopped
     4 thin slices rye bread, crust removed
     8 ounces sliced Swiss cheese
     8 ounces sliced cooked corned beef or pastrami

1. Combine HELLMANN'S® or BEST FOODS® Real Mayonnaise, WISH-BONE® Thousand Island Dressing and sauerkraut in medium bowl; set aside.

2. Top 2 bread slices evenly with cheese, corned beef, then remaining bread. Cut each sandwich into 20 cubes and secure with wooden toothpicks. Serve with dipping sauce.   *Makes 40 servings*

Prep Time: 10 minutes

Velveeta® Double-Decker Nachos

  6 ounces tortilla chips (about 7 cups)
  1 can (15 ounces) chili with beans
½ pound (8 ounces) VELVEETA® Pasteurized Prepared Cheese Product,
    cut into ½-inch cubes
  1 medium tomato, finely chopped
¼ cup sliced green onions
⅓ cup BREAKSTONE'S® or KNUDSEN® Sour Cream

1. ARRANGE half of the chips on large microwavable platter; top with layers of half each of the chili and VELVEETA®. Repeat layers.

2. MICROWAVE on HIGH 3 to 5 minutes or until VELVEETA® is melted.

3. TOP with remaining ingredients.   *Makes 6 servings.*

Substitution: Prepare as directed, using VELVEETA® Mild Mexican Pasteurized Prepared Cheese Product with Jalapeño Peppers.

Prep Time: 15 minutes

 Tip   Cut VELVEETA® loaf into ½-inch-thick
slices, then cut each slice crosswise in
both directions to make cubes.

Quirky Bites

Summer Salad Lettuce Wraps

¼ cup olive oil
    Juice of 1 lime
 1 tablespoon red wine vinegar
 1 cup grape tomatoes, halved
 1 cup corn
½ cup diced fresh mozzarella cheese
¼ cup diced red onion
¼ cup chopped fresh basil leaves
    Salt and black pepper
 6 crunchy lettuce leaves

1. Whisk oil, lime juice and vinegar in large bowl.

2. Add tomatoes, corn, cheese, onion and basil; toss to coat. Season with salt and pepper.

3. To serve, scoop ¼ cup salad mixture onto each lettuce leaf.

Makes 3 servings

Heavenly Ham Roll-Ups

1 package (9 ounces) OSCAR MAYER® Shaved Smoked Ham
5 tablespoons PHILADELPHIA® Light Cream Cheese Spread
15 asparagus spears (about 1 pound), trimmed

PREHEAT oven to 350°F. Flatten ham slices; pat dry. Stack ham in piles of 2 slices each; spread each stack with 1 teaspoon of the cream cheese spread.

PLACE 1 asparagus spear on one of the long sides of each ham stack; roll up. Place in 13×9-inch baking dish.

BAKE 15 to 20 minutes or until heated through.   *Makes 15 servings*

Prep Time: 15 minutes
Bake Time: 15 to 20 minutes

Hot and Spicy Hummus Dip

1 container (8 ounces) prepared hummus
½ cup mayonnaise
2 to 3 tablespoons chipotle salsa*
1 tablespoon minced green onion
   Pita chips and/or vegetables

Chipotle salsa is a canned mixture of finely chopped chipotle peppers in adobo sauce. Look for it in the Latin foods section of the supermarket.

1. Combine hummus, mayonnaise, salsa and green onion in medium bowl. Cover and refrigerate until ready to serve.

2. Serve with pita chips.   *Makes about 6 servings*

Serving Suggestion: Use this spicy dip to liven up sandwiches or wraps.

Guacamole Cones

6 (6-inch) flour tortillas
1 tablespoon vegetable oil
1 teaspoon chili powder
2 ripe avocados
1½ tablespoons fresh lime juice
1 tablespoon finely chopped green onion
¼ teaspoon salt
¼ teaspoon black pepper
Dash hot pepper sauce (optional)
2 to 3 plum tomatoes, chopped

1. Preheat oven to 350°F. Line baking sheet with parchment paper.

2. Cut tortillas in half. Roll each tortilla half into cone shape; secure with toothpick. Brush outside of each cone with oil; sprinkle lightly with chili powder. Place on prepared baking sheet.

3. Bake 9 minutes or until lightly browned. Turn cones upside down; bake 5 minutes or until golden brown on all sides. Cool 1 minute; remove toothpicks and cool completely.

4. Cut avocados in half; remove and discard pits. Scoop out pulp and place in medium bowl; mash with fork. Stir in lime juice, green onion, salt, black pepper and hot pepper sauce, if desired.

5. Fill bottom of each tortilla cone with 1 tablespoon chopped tomato; top with small scoop of guacamole and additional chopped tomatoes. Serve immediately. *Makes 12 cones*

Bavarian Pretzel Sandwiches

4 frozen soft pretzels, thawed
1 tablespoon German mustard
2 teaspoons mayonnaise
8 slices Black Forest ham
4 slices Gouda cheese
1 tablespoon water
  Coarse salt

1. Preheat oven to 350°F. Line baking sheet with parchment paper.

2. Carefully slice each pretzel in half crosswise using serrated knife. Combine mustard and mayonnaise in small bowl. Spread mustard mixture onto bottom halves of pretzels. Top with 2 slices ham, 1 slice cheese and top halves of pretzels.

3. Place sandwiches on prepared baking sheet. Brush tops of sandwiches with water; sprinkle with salt. Bake 8 minutes or until cheese is melted.

Makes 4 sandwiches

Crispy Bacon Sticks

½ cup (1½ ounces) grated Wisconsin Parmesan cheese, divided
5 slices bacon, halved lengthwise
10 breadsticks

Microwave Directions

Spread ¼ cup cheese on plate. Press one side of bacon into cheese; wrap diagonally around breadstick with cheese-coated side toward stick. Place on paper plate or microwave-safe baking sheet lined with paper towels. Repeat with remaining bacon halves, cheese and breadsticks. Microwave on HIGH 4 to 6 minutes or until bacon is cooked, checking for doneness after 4 minutes. Roll again in remaining ¼ cup Parmesan cheese. Serve warm.

Makes 10 sticks

Favorite recipe from Wisconsin Milk Marketing Board

Great Zukes Pizza Bites

 1 medium zucchini
 3 tablespoons pizza sauce
 2 tablespoons tomato paste
 ¼ teaspoon dried oregano
 ¾ cup (3 ounces) shredded mozzarella cheese
 ¼ cup shredded Parmesan cheese
 8 slices pitted black olives
 8 slices pepperoni

1. Preheat broiler; set rack 4 inches from heat source.

2. Trim off and discard ends of zucchini. Cut zucchini into 16 (¼-inch-thick) diagonal slices. Place on nonstick baking sheet.

3. Combine pizza sauce, tomato paste and oregano in small bowl; mix well. Spread scant teaspoon sauce over each zucchini slice. Combine cheeses in small bowl. Top each zucchini slice with 1 tablespoon cheese mixture, pressing down into sauce. Place 1 olive slice on each of 8 pizza bites. Place 1 folded pepperoni slice on each remaining pizza bite.

4. Broil 3 minutes or until cheese is melted. Serve immediately.

Makes 8 servings

 Tip For a vegetarian option, substitute sliced mushrooms for pepperoni.

California Ham Rolls

  2 cups water
½ teaspoon salt, divided
  1 cup short grain brown rice
  2 tablespoons Asian rice vinegar* or cider vinegar
  1 tablespoon sugar
  4 (8-inch) sheets nori (sushi wrappers)*
  8 thin strips ham (about 4 ounces)
¼ cup reduced-sodium soy sauce
  1 tablespoon mirin (sweet rice wine)*
  1 tablespoon minced chives

*These ingredients can be found in the ethnic section of your supermarket.

1. Bring water and ¼ teaspoon salt to a boil in medium saucepan over high heat. Stir in rice. Cover and reduce heat to low. Simmer 40 minutes or until water is absorbed and rice is tender but chewy. Spoon into large shallow bowl.

2. Combine vinegar, sugar and remaining ¼ teaspoon salt in small bowl. Microwave on HIGH 30 seconds. Stir to dissolve sugar. Pour over rice, stirring to mix well. Set aside to cool.

3. Place 1 sheet nori on work surface. Loosely spread about ½ cup rice over nori, leaving ½-inch border. Place 2 strips ham along width of nori. Roll up tightly into an 8-inch tube. Gently press tube to redistribute rice, if necessary. Cut tube into 6 slices with sharp knife. Place cut side up on serving plate. Repeat with remaining nori, rice and ham.

4. Combine soy sauce and mirin in small bowl. Sprinkle with chives. Serve with ham rolls for dipping.   *Makes 24 appetizers*

Bell Pepper Wedges with Herbed Goat Cheese

  2 red bell peppers
  1 package (4 ounces) goat cheese, softened
  ⅓ cup whipped cream cheese
  2 tablespoons minced fresh chives
  1 teaspoon minced fresh dill
    Fresh dill sprigs (optional)

1. Cut off top quarter of bell peppers; remove core and seeds. Cut each pepper into 6 wedges. Remove ribs, if necessary.

2. Combine goat cheese, cream cheese, chives and minced dill in small bowl until well blended. Pipe or spread 1 tablespoon goat cheese mixture onto each pepper wedge. Garnish with dill sprigs, if desired.   *Makes 6 servings*

Bite-You-Back Roasted Edamame

  2 teaspoons vegetable oil
  2 teaspoons honey
  ¼ teaspoon wasabi powder*
  1 package (10 ounces) shelled edamame, thawed if frozen
    Kosher salt (optional)

This ingredient can be found in the Asian section of most supermarkets and in Asian specialty markets.

1. Preheat oven to 375°F.

2. Whisk oil, honey and wasabi powder in large bowl until well blended. Add edamame; toss to coat. Spread in single layer on baking sheet.

3. Bake 12 minutes or until golden brown, stirring once. Immediately transfer to large bowl; sprinkle generously with salt, if desired. Cool completely before serving. Store in airtight container.   *Makes 4 to 6 servings*

Spicy Polenta Cheese Bites

  3 cups water

  1 cup corn grits or cornmeal

½ teaspoon salt

¼ teaspoon chili powder

  1 tablespoon butter

¼ cup minced onion or shallot

  1 tablespoon minced jalapeño pepper*

½ cup (2 ounces) shredded sharp Cheddar or fontina cheese

Jalapeño peppers can sting and irritate the skin, so wear rubber gloves when handling peppers and do not touch your eyes.

1. Grease 8-inch square baking pan. Bring water to a boil in large nonstick saucepan over high heat. Slowly add grits, stirring constantly. Reduce heat to low; cook and stir until grits are tender and water is absorbed. Stir in salt and chili powder. Remove from heat.

2. Melt butter in small saucepan over medium-high heat. Add onion and jalapeño; cook and stir 3 to 5 minutes or until tender. Stir into grits; mix well. Spread in prepared pan. Let stand 1 hour or until cool and firm.

3. Preheat broiler. Cut polenta into 16 squares. Arrange squares on nonstick baking sheet; sprinkle with cheese. Broil 4 inches from heat source 5 minutes or until cheese is melted and slightly browned. Remove immediately. Cut squares in half. Serve warm or at room temperature.   *Makes 32 appetizers*

 **Tip** For spicier flavor, add ⅛ teaspoon red pepper flakes to the onion-jalapeño pepper mixture.

Porky Pinwheels

1 sheet frozen puff pastry, thawed
1 egg white, beaten
8 slices bacon, crisp-cooked and crumbled
2 tablespoons packed brown sugar
¼ teaspoon ground red pepper

1. Place pastry on sheet of parchment paper. Brush with egg white.

2. Combine bacon, brown sugar and red pepper in small bowl. Sprinkle evenly over top of pastry, pressing lightly to adhere. Roll pastry jelly-roll style from long end. Wrap in parchment paper. Refrigerate 30 minutes.

3. Preheat oven to 400°F. Line baking sheet with parchment paper. Slice pastry into ½-inch-thick slices. Place 1 inch apart on prepared baking sheet.

4. Bake 10 minutes or until light golden brown. Remove to wire racks; cool completely.   *Makes 24 pinwheels*

Parmesan-Pepper Crisps

2 cups (4 ounces) coarsely grated Parmesan cheese
2 teaspoons black pepper

1. Preheat oven to 400°F. Line wire racks with paper towels.

2. Place heaping teaspoonfuls cheese 2 inches apart on ungreased nonstick baking sheet. Flatten cheese mounds slightly with back of spoon. Sprinkle each mound with pinch of pepper.

3. Bake 15 minutes or until crisps are very lightly browned. (Watch closely because crisps burn easily.) Cool on baking sheet 2 minutes. Carefully remove with spatula to prepared racks to cool completely. Store in airtight container in refrigerator up to 3 days.   *Makes about 26 crisps*

Kiddie Creations

Pig-wich

Mayonnaise or mustard
2 round slices deli meat
1½ round cheese slices, divided
1 leaf Boston lettuce
1 round sandwich bun, split
1 black olive
1 slice bologna
1 black bean

1. Layer mayonnaise, deli meat, 1 slice cheese and lettuce on bottom half of bun. Spread mayonnaise on cut side of top half of bun and place slightly off center on top of lettuce. Slice olive in half lengthwise, then cut small V shape out of bottom of each half. Place olive halves on lettuce, cut sides facing out, for feet.

2. Cut circle from bologna with round cutter for snout. Cut two small holes in circle just above center for nostrils. Using mayonnaise, attach circle to top bun. Cut two triangles from bologna. Make two slits in top half of bun 1 inch apart and angling slightly towards sides of bun. Insert triangles into slits for ears.

3. Cut out two small circles from remaining ½ slice cheese; using mayonnaise, attach to bun between ears and nose for eyes. Cut black bean in half; attach cut sides to cheese circle for pupils. Cut long tapered slice of bologna. Attach to side of pig and curl for tail.   *Makes 1 sandwich*

Breakfast Mice

2 hard-cooked eggs, peeled and halved lengthwise
2 teaspoons mayonnaise
¼ teaspoon salt
2 radishes, thinly sliced and root ends reserved
8 raisins or currants
1 ounce Cheddar cheese, shredded or cubed

1. Gently scoop egg yolks into small bowl. Mash yolks, mayonnaise and salt until smooth. Spoon yolk mixture back into egg halves. Place two halves, cut side down, on each serving plate.

2. Cut two tiny slits near the narrow end of each egg half; position 2 radish slices on each half for ears. Use the root end of each radish to form tails. Push raisins into each egg half to form eyes. Place small pile of cheese in front of each mouse.

Makes 2 servings

Candy Corn by the Slice

1 package (about 14 ounces) refrigerated pizza crust dough
½ cup (2 ounces) shredded mozzarella cheese
2 cups (8 ounces) shredded Cheddar cheese, divided
⅓ cup pizza sauce

1. Preheat oven to 400°F. Spray 13-inch round pizza pan with nonstick cooking spray. Press dough into pan.

2. Sprinkle mozzarella in 4-inch circle in center of pizza dough. Sprinkle 1 cup Cheddar cheese in 3-inch ring around center circle. Spoon pizza sauce over Cheddar cheese. Create 1½-inch border around edge of pizza with remaining 1 cup Cheddar cheese.

3. Bake 12 minutes or until edge is lightly browned and cheese is melted. Cut into wedges.

Makes 8 slices

Magic Rainbow Pops

    1 envelope (¼ ounce) unflavored gelatin
¼ cup cold water
½ cup boiling water
    1 container (6 ounces) raspberry or strawberry yogurt
    1 container (6 ounces) lemon or orange yogurt
    1 can (8¼ ounces) apricots or peaches with juice
    Pop molds

1. Combine gelatin and cold water in 2-cup glass measuring cup. Let stand 5 minutes to soften. Add boiling water. Stir until gelatin is completely dissolved. Cool to room temperature.

2. Combine raspberry yogurt and ¼ cup gelatin mixture in small bowl; stir until completely blended. Fill each pop mold about one third full with raspberry mixture.* Freeze 30 to 60 minutes or until set.

3. Combine lemon yogurt with ¼ cup gelatin mixture in small bowl; stir until completely blended. Pour lemon mixture over raspberry layer in each mold.* Freeze 30 to 60 minutes or until set.

4. Place apricots with juice and remaining ¼ cup gelatin mixture in blender or food processor; blend 20 seconds or until smooth. Pour apricot mixture evenly into molds.* Cover with lids. Freeze 2 to 5 hours or until firm.

5. To remove pops from molds, place bottoms of pops under warm running water until loosened. Press firmly on bottoms to release. (Do not twist or pull sticks.)   *Makes about 6 pops*

Pour any extra mixture into small paper cups. Freeze as directed in the tip.

Tip: Three-ounce paper cups can be used in place of the molds. Make the layers as directed or put a single flavor in each cup. Freeze cups about 1 hour, then insert wooden stick (which can be found at craft stores) into the center of each cup. Freeze completely. Peel cup off each pop to serve.

Great Green Veggie Wedgies

½ cup whipped cream cheese
2 (8- to 10-inch) spinach tortillas
¼ cup apricot or peach fruit spread
½ cup coarsely chopped fresh baby spinach
¼ cup grated carrot

1. Evenly spread cream cheese over one side of each tortilla.

2. Spread fruit spread over cream cheese on 1 tortilla. Arrange spinach and carrots over fruit spread.

3. Place the second tortilla, cheese side down, on top of the spinach and carrots. Lightly press tortillas together. To serve, cut into wedges.

Makes 2 servings

Bagel Dogs with Spicy Red Sauce

1 cup ketchup
1 onion, finely chopped
¼ cup packed brown sugar
1 tablespoon cider vinegar
2 teaspoons hot pepper sauce
1 clove garlic, minced
1 teaspoon Worcestershire sauce
1 teaspoon liquid smoke (optional)
4 bagel dogs

1. Combine ketchup, onion, brown sugar, vinegar, hot pepper sauce, garlic, Worcestershire sauce and liquid smoke, if desired, in medium saucepan. Bring to a boil over medium-high heat. Reduce heat; simmer 5 minutes, stirring occasionally.

2. Prepare bagel dogs according to package directions. Serve with sauce for dipping.

Makes 4 servings

Bird-wich

Mayonnaise or mustard
2 round slices deli meat
2 round slices white cheese
1 round sandwich bun, split
2 leaves romaine lettuce
2 slices black olive
2 peas
1 slice yellow cheese
Parsley sprigs (optional)

1. Layer mayonnaise, deli meat and 1 slice white cheese on bottom half of bun. Cut circle out of front end of top bun with round cutter, angling towards center. Spread mayonnaise on cut side of top bun and place on top of cheese.

2. Insert 2 lettuce leaves between cheese and top bun on opposite sides of sandwich for wings. Cut remaining slice white cheese in half. Loosely roll one half; roll other half slightly tighter and insert into looser half. Insert into hole in bun for beak.

3. Insert peas into holes in olive slices. Using mayonnaise, attach to bun above beak for eyes. Cut two triangles from yellow cheese for feet. Cut two small V shapes out of short side of each triangle. Slide feet under sandwich, cut sides out.

4. Top sandwich with parsley sprigs for feathers. *Makes 1 sandwich*

Snake Snacks

2 small bananas
1 tablespoon fresh lemon juice
10 to 12 medium strawberries, hulled
2 small strawberries, hulled
1 slice kiwi (optional)

1. Cut bananas crosswise into ¼-inch slices. Place in medium bowl; toss gently with lemon juice to prevent bananas from turning brown.

2. Leave 2 medium strawberries whole; cut remaining medium strawberries crosswise into ¼-inch slices.

3. Place whole strawberries on serving plates for heads; arrange bananas and strawberry slices in alternating pattern behind heads to form snakes. Arrange small strawberries at ends of snakes.

4. Cut four small pieces of banana for eyes; arrange on snake heads. Use toothpick to place kiwi seed in center of each eye, if desired.

Makes 2 servings

 Tip Try to choose strawberries that are about the same diameter as the banana so all the fruit slices that make up the snake will be close to the same width.

Friendly Face Pizzas

    3 whole wheat English muffins, split in half
    ¾ cup pasta sauce
    ¾ cup (3 ounces) shredded Italian cheese blend
       Assorted vegetables

1. Preheat oven to 400°F. Place muffin halves on baking sheet.

2. Spread pasta sauce onto muffins. Sprinkle with cheese. Using vegetables, create silly faces on top of cheese.

3. Bake 8 to 10 minutes or until cheese is melted.   *Makes 6 servings*

Indian Corn

    ¼ cup (½ stick) butter or margarine
    1 package (10½ ounces) mini marshmallows
       Yellow food coloring
    8 cups peanut butter and chocolate puffed corn cereal
    1 cup candy-coated chocolate pieces, divided
   10 lollipop sticks
       Tan and green raffia

1. Line baking sheet with waxed paper.

2. Melt butter in large heavy saucepan over low heat. Add marshmallows; cook and stir until melted and smooth. Add food coloring, a few drops at a time, until desired shade is reached. Add cereal and ½ cup chocolate pieces; stir until evenly coated. Remove from heat.

3. With lightly greased hands, quickly divide mixture into 10 oblong pieces. Push lollipop stick halfway into each piece; shape like ear of corn. Place on prepared baking sheet. Press remaining ½ cup chocolate pieces into each ear. Let stand until set.

4. Tie or tape raffia to lollipop sticks to resemble corn husks.

Makes 10 servings

Chocolate Goldfish® Pretzel Clusters

1 package (12 ounces) semi-sweet chocolate pieces (about 2 cups)
2½ cups PEPPERIDGE FARM® Pretzel Goldfish® Crackers
1 container (4 ounces) multi-colored nonpareils

1. Line a baking sheet with wax paper.

2. Place the chocolate into a microwavable bowl. Microwave on MEDIUM for 30 seconds. Stir. Repeat until the chocolate is melted and smooth. Add the Goldfish® crackers and stir to coat.

3. Drop the chocolate mixture by tablespoonfuls onto the baking sheet. Sprinkle the clusters with the nonpareils.

4. Refrigerate for 30 minutes or until the clusters are firm. Keep refrigerated until ready to serve.   *Makes 24 servings*

Prep Time: 5 minutes
Cook Time: 1 minute
Chill Time: 30 minutes

 Tip To wrap for gift-giving, arrange the clusters in a small box lined with colored plastic wrap.

Sweet Surprises

Chocolate-Covered Banana Pops

   3 ripe large bananas
   9 wooden popsicle sticks
   2 cups (12-ounce package) HERSHEY'S SPECIAL DARK® Chocolate
       Chips or HERSHEY'S Semi-Sweet Chocolate Chips
   2 tablespoons shortening (do not use butter, margarine, spread or oil)
1½ cups coarsely chopped unsalted, roasted peanuts

1. Peel bananas; cut each into thirds. Insert a wooden stick into each banana piece; place on wax paper-covered tray. Cover; freeze until firm.

2. Place chocolate chips and shortening in medium microwave-safe bowl. Microwave at MEDIUM (50%) 1½ to 2 minutes or until chocolate is melted and mixture is smooth when stirred.

3. Remove bananas from freezer just before dipping. Dip each piece into warm chocolate, covering completely; allow excess to drip off. Immediately roll in peanuts. Cover; return to freezer. Serve frozen.   *Makes 9 pops*

Variation: HERSHEY'S Milk Chocolate Chips or HERSHEY'S Mini Chips Semi-Sweet Chocolate may be substituted for HERSHEY'S SPECIAL DARK Chocolate Chips or HERSHEY'S Semi-Sweet Chocolate Chips.

Mini S'mores Pies

   6 mini graham cracker pie crusts
   ½ cup semisweet chocolate chips, divided
   ¾ cup mini marshmallows

1. Preheat oven to 325°F. Place pie crusts on baking sheet.

2. Evenly divide ¼ cup chocolate chips among pie crusts. Sprinkle marshmallows over chocolate chips. Top with remaining ¼ cup chocolate chips.

3. Bake 3 to 5 minutes or until marshmallows are light golden brown. Serve warm.

Makes 6 servings

Pound Cake Dip Sticks

   ½ cup raspberry jam, divided
     1 package (10¾ ounces) frozen pound cake
   1½ cups cold whipping cream

1. Preheat oven to 400°F. Spray baking sheet with nonstick cooking spray.

2. Microwave ¼ cup jam on HIGH 20 to 30 seconds or until slightly softened and smooth. Cut pound cake into 10 (½-inch) slices. Brush one side of slices with warm jam. Cut each slice lengthwise into three sticks. Place sticks, jam side up, on prepared baking sheet.

3. Bake 10 minutes or until cake sticks are crisp and light golden brown. Remove to wire rack; cool completely.

4. Meanwhile, beat cream in large bowl with electric mixer at high speed until soft peaks form. Add remaining ¼ cup raspberry jam; beat until combined. Serve dip sticks with raspberry whipped cream for dipping.

Makes 8 to 10 servings

Mini Dessert Burgers

  1 box (12 ounces) vanilla wafer cookies,* divided
  ½ cup powdered sugar
  ¼ teaspoon salt
  ¾ cup NESTLÉ® TOLL HOUSE® Semi-Sweet Chocolate Morsels
  ⅓ cup milk
  ½ cup sweetened flaked coconut
  ½ teaspoon water
  3 drops green food coloring
     Red and yellow decorating gels
  1 teaspoon melted butter (optional)
  1 tablespoon sesame seeds (optional)

*A 12-ounce box of vanilla wafers contains about 88 wafers.

RESERVE 48 wafers for bun tops and bottoms.

PLACE remaining wafers in large resealable bag. Crush into small pieces using a rolling pin. Combine wafer crumbs (about 1½ cups) with powdered sugar and salt in medium bowl.

MICROWAVE morsels and milk in medium, uncovered, microwave-safe bowl on high (100%) power for 45 seconds; Stir. If necessary, microwave at additional 10- to 15-second intervals, stirring just until smooth.

POUR chocolate mixture into wafer mixture; stir until combined. Cool for 10 minutes. Line baking sheet with wax paper. Roll mixture into 24, 1-inch (about 1 tablespoon each) balls. Place each ball on prepared sheet; flatten slightly to form burger patties.

COMBINE coconut, water and green food coloring in small, resealable plastic bag. Seal bag and shake to coat evenly with color.

PLACE 24 wafers, rounded side down on prepared baking sheet. Top each wafer with 1 burger patty. Top each burger patty with 1 teaspoon colored coconut. Squeeze decorating gels on top of coconut. Top with remaining wafers. Brush tops of wafers with melted butter and sprinkle with sesame seeds, if desired.   *Makes 24 servings*

Tip: Recipe can easily be doubled or tripled. Great birthday or slumber party activity.

Chocolate Panini Bites

    ¼ cup chocolate hazelnut spread
    4 slices hearty sandwich bread or Italian bread
      Nonstick cooking spray

1. Preheat indoor grill.* Spread chocolate hazelnut spread evenly over 2 bread slices. Top with remaining bread slices.

2. Spray both sides of sandwiches with nonstick cooking spray. Grill 2 to 3 minutes per side or until golden brown. To serve, cut sandwiches into triangles. *Makes 4 servings*

Panini can also be made on the stove in a ridged grill pan or in a nonstick skillet. Cook sandwiches over medium heat about 2 minutes per side.

Chocolate Raspberry Panini Bites: Spread 2 bread slices with raspberry jam or preserves. Spread remaining bread slices with chocolate hazelnut spread. Cook sandwiches as directed above. Watch grill or pan closely because jam burns easily.

S'more Snack Cake

    1 package (about 18 ounces) yellow cake mix, plus ingredients
        to prepare mix
    1 cup chocolate chunks, divided
  2½ cups bear-shaped graham crackers, divided
  1½ cups mini marshmallows

1. Preheat oven to 350°F. Grease 13×9-inch baking pan.

2. Prepare cake mix according to package directions. Stir in ½ cup chocolate chunks and 1 cup graham crackers. Pour batter in prepared pan.

3. Bake 30 minutes. Sprinkle with remaining ½ cup chocolate chunks and marshmallows. Arrange remaining 1½ cups graham crackers evenly over top.

4. Bake 8 minutes or until marshmallows are golden brown. Cool completely before cutting. *Makes 24 servings*

Note: This cake is best served the day it is made.

Drizzled Party Popcorn

8 cups popped popcorn
½ cup HERSHEY'S Milk Chocolate Chips
2 teaspoons shortening (do not use butter, margarine, spread or oil), divided
½ cup REESE'S® Peanut Butter Chips

1. Line cookie sheet or jelly-roll pan with wax paper. Spread popcorn in thin layer on prepared pan.

2. Place milk chocolate chips and 1 teaspoon shortening in microwave-safe bowl. Microwave at MEDIUM (50%) 30 seconds; stir. If necessary, microwave at MEDIUM an additional 10 seconds at a time, stirring after each heating, until chips are melted and smooth when stirred. Drizzle over popcorn.

3. Place peanut butter chips and remaining 1 teaspoon shortening in separate microwave-safe bowl. Microwave at MEDIUM 30 seconds; stir. If necessary, microwave at MEDIUM an additional 10 seconds at a time, stirring after each heating, until chips are melted and smooth when stirred. Drizzle over popcorn.

4. Allow drizzle to set up at room temperature or refrigerate about 10 minutes or until firm. Break popcorn into pieces. *Makes about 8 cups popcorn*

Notes: Popcorn is best eaten the same day as prepared, but it can be stored in an airtight container. Recipe amounts can be changed to match your personal preferences.

Sweet Sushi

1 package (about 10 ounces) marshmallows
3 tablespoons butter
6 cups crisp rice cereal
  Green fruit roll-ups
  Sliced strawberries, peaches and kiwi
  Candy fish

1. Spray 13×9-inch baking pan and spatula with nonstick cooking spray.

2. Place marshmallows and butter in large microwavable bowl; microwave on HIGH 1 to 2 minutes or until melted and smooth, stirring once. Immediately stir in cereal until evenly coated. Press mixture into prepared pan, using waxed paper to press into even layer, if necessary. Let stand 10 minutes to set.

3. Cut half of cereal treat into 2×1-inch rectangles; round edges of rectangles slightly to form ovals. Cut remaining half of treat into 1½- to 2-inch circles, using greased cookie or biscuit cutter.

4. Cut fruit roll-ups into ½-inch-wide and 1-inch-wide strips. Top oval pieces with candy or fruit; wrap with ½-inch fruit roll-up strips around ovals as shown in photo. Wrap 1-inch strips around sides of circle pieces. Top with fruit or candy.   *Makes 3 to 4 dozen pieces*

Marty the "Mousse"

2 packages (8 squares each) BAKER'S® Semi-Sweet Chocolate, divided
1 package (8 ounces) PHILADELPHIA® Cream Cheese, softened
½ cup PLANTERS® Walnut Halves
   Decorations: red candy-coated chocolate pieces and small candies

MELT 8 chocolate squares. Beat cream cheese with electric mixer until creamy. Blend in melted chocolate. Refrigerate 1 hour or until firm.

SHAPE into 18 balls, using 4 teaspoons chocolate mixture for each; place in single layer on waxed paper-covered baking sheet.

MELT remaining chocolate squares. Dip balls in chocolate, 1 at a time, turning to evenly coat each ball. Return to baking sheet.

PRESS 2 nuts into top of each ball for the moose's antlers. Add decorations for the nose and eyes. Refrigerate until chocolate is firm.   *Makes 18 servings*

Special Extra: Add 1 to 2 teaspoons of your favorite extract, such as peppermint, rum or almond, to chocolate mixture before shaping into balls.

Prep Time: 20 minutes (plus refrigerating)

Pretzel Fried Eggs

24 (1-inch) pretzel rings
1 cup white chocolate chips
24 yellow candy-coated chocolate pieces

1. Line baking sheet with waxed paper. Place pretzel rings about 2 inches apart on prepared baking sheet.

2. Place white chocolate chips in medium resealable food storage bag; seal bag. Microwave on HIGH 30 seconds. Turn bag over; heat on HIGH at 30-second intervals or until chocolate is melted. Knead bag until chocolate is smooth. Cut off tiny corner of bag.

3. Squeeze chocolate into center of each pretzel ring in circular motion. Finish with ring of chocolate around edge of pretzel. Use tip of small knife to smooth chocolate, if necessary. Place candy piece in center of each pretzel. Let stand at room temperature until firm. Store in single layer in airtight container up to 1 week.

Makes 2 dozen eggs

 **Tip** To make "green eggs and ham," use green candy-coated chocolate pieces for yolks. Cut small pieces of pink fruit leather for ham. Serve 2 Pretzel Fried Eggs with small strips of fruit leather ham and square cinnamon cereal for toast.

Banana Split Cups

1 package (18 ounces) refrigerated chocolate chip cookie dough
⅔ cup "M&M's"® Chocolate Mini Baking Bits, divided
1 ripe medium banana, cut into 18 slices and halved
¾ cup chocolate syrup, divided
2¼ cups any flavor ice cream, softened
Aerosol whipped topping
¼ cup chopped maraschino cherries

Lightly grease 36 (1¾-inch) mini muffin cups. Cut dough into 36 equal pieces; roll into balls. Place 1 ball in bottom of each muffin cup. Press dough onto bottoms and up sides of muffin cups; chill 15 minutes. Press ⅓ cup "M&M's"® Chocolate Mini Baking Bits into bottoms and sides of dough cups. Preheat oven to 350°F. Bake cookies 8 to 9 minutes. Cookies will be puffy. Remove from oven; gently press down center of each cookie. Return to oven 1 minute. Cool cookies in muffin cups 5 minutes. Remove to wire racks; cool completely. Place 1 banana half slice in each cookie cup; top with ½ teaspoon chocolate syrup. Place about ½ teaspoon "M&M's"® Chocolate Mini Baking Bits in each cookie cup; top with 1 tablespoon ice cream. Top each cookie cup with ½ teaspoon chocolate syrup, whipped topping, remaining "M&M's"® Chocolate Mini Baking Bits and 1 maraschino cherry piece. Store covered in freezer.

Makes 3 dozen cookies

The publisher would like to thank the companies and organizations listed below for the use of their recipes and photographs in this publication.

Campbell Soup Company

Dole Food Company, Inc.

Heinz North America

The Hershey Company

Kraft Foods Global, Inc.

© Mars, Incorporated 2011

Nestlé USA

Ortega®, A Division of B&G Foods, Inc.

The Quaker® Oatmeal Kitchens

Unilever

Wisconsin Milk Marketing Board

A

Angelic Cupcakes, 46
Apple
    Taffy Apple Cupcakes, 28
    Tuna Schooners, 208
Avocado
    Guacamole Cones, 232
    Guacamole Sliders, 220

B

Bacon
    BLT Biscuits, 204
    Crispy Bacon Sticks, 234
    Hawaiian Pizza Bites, 196
    Porky Pinwheels, 244
Bagel Dogs with Spicy Red Sauce, 252
Baked Pork Buns, 222
Banana
    Banana Cupcakes, 70
    Banana Split Cups, 278
    Chocolate-Covered Banana Pops, 262
    Snake Snacks, 256
    Whirlgigs, 188
Banana Cupcakes, 70
Banana Split Cups, 278
Bavarian Pretzel Sandwiches, 234
Beans
    Bite-You-Back Roasted Edamame, 240
    Hot Cheesy Chili Dip, 214
    Velveeta® Double-Decker Nachos, 226
Beef
    Beer-Braised Meatballs, 216
    Guacamole Sliders, 220
    Hot Cheesy Chili Dip, 214
    Meat Loaf Cupcakes, 198
    Mini Reuben Skewers with Dipping Sauce, 224
    Sloppy Joe Sliders, 206
Beer & Spirits
    Beer-Braised Meatballs, 216
    Margarita Cupcakes, 52
    Mini Tiramisu Cupcakes, 86

Beer-Braised Meatballs, 216
Bell Pepper Wedges with Herbed Goat Cheese, 240
Berry
    Blueberry Cheesecake Cupcakes, 68
    Chocolate Raspberry Panini Bites, 268
    Chocolate Sweetheart Cupcakes, 18
    Magic Rainbow Pops, 250
    Peanut Butter Aliens, 118
    Peanut Butter & Jelly Cupcakes, 60
    Pound Cake Dip Sticks, 264
    Raspberry Streusel Cupcakes, 74
    Snake Snacks, 256
    Strawberry Short Cupcakes, 78
    Whirlgigs, 188
    Window-to-My-Heart Cookies, 170
Billiard Balls, 138
Bird-wich, 254
Birthday Cake Cookies, 162
Bite-You-Back Roasted Edamame, 240
Black Bottom Cupcakes, 90
BLT Biscuits, 204
Blueberry Cheesecake Cupcakes, 68
Breakfast Mice, 248
Brownie Mix
    Mighty Milkshakes, 158
    Mini Turtle Cupcakes, 82
    Treasure Chests, 128
Buffalo Wedges, 214
Building Blocks, 124
Burger Bliss, 156
Buttercream Frosting, 8, 176

C

Cake Mix
    Angelic Cupcakes, 46
    Chocolate Easter Baskets, 22
    Chocolate Sweetheart Cupcakes, 18
    Colorful Caterpillar Cupcakes, 8
    Dinocakes, 4
    Dragonflies, 44
    Easy Easter Cupcakes, 20
    Fairy Tale Cupcakes, 34
    Fishy Friends, 10

Cake Mix *(continued)*
Friendly Frogs, 36
Fudgy Mocha Cupcakes with
    Chocolate Coffee Ganache, 92
Graduation Party Cupcakes, 24
Hedgehogs, 6
Hot Chocolate Cupcakes, 62
Key Lime Pie Cupcakes, 66
Lemon Meringue Cupcakes, 76
Little Lamb Cakes, 14
Margarita Cupcakes, 52
Marshmallow Fudge Sundae
    Cupcakes, 56
Mini Doughnut Cupcakes, 64
Mini Mice, 2
Mini Tiramisu Cupcakes, 86
Panda Cupcakes, 16
Pink Lemonade Cupcakes, 72
Rocky Road Cupcakes, 88
S'more Snack Cake, 268
Sunny Side Upcakes, 48
Surprise Package Cupcakes, 26
Sweet Snowmen, 32
Tasty Turtles, 100
Under the Sea, 40
California Ham Rolls, 238
Candy Corn by the Slice, 248
Caramel
Lollipop Flower Pots, 178
Mini Turtle Cupcakes, 82
Taffy Apple Cupcakes, 28
Cereal
Indian Corn, 258
Sweet Sushi, 272
Cheery Chocolate Animal Cookies, 121
Cheese *(see also* Cream Cheese)
Bavarian Pretzel Sandwiches, 234
Beer-Braised Meatballs, 216
Bell Pepper Wedges with Herbed
    Goat Cheese, 240
Bird-wich, 254
BLT Biscuits, 204
Candy Corn by the Slice, 248
Chili Cheese Mini Dogs, 224
Crispy Bacon Sticks, 234

Cheese *(continued)*
Croque Monsieur Bites, 210
Friendly Face Pizzas, 258
Great Zukes Pizza Bites, 236
Grilled Cheese Kabobs, 196
Hawaiian Pizza Bites, 196
Heavenly Ham Roll-Ups, 230
Hot Cheesy Chili Dip, 214
Italian Chicken Nuggets, 202
Mac and Cheese Mini Cups, 200
Micro Mini Stuffed Potatoes, 194
Mini Reuben Skewers with Dipping
    Sauce, 224
Parmesan Pepper Crisps, 244
Pig-wich, 246
Pizza Fries, 218
Poblano Pepper Kabobs, 218
Spicy Polenta Cheese Bites, 242
Summer Salad Lettuce Wraps, 228
Turkey Club Biscuits
Velveeta® Double-Decker Nachos,
    226
Chicken & Turkey
Italian Chicken Nuggets, 202
Poblano Pepper Kabobs, 218
Turkey Club Biscuits, 204
Chili Cheese Mini Dogs, 224
Chocolate *(see also* Chocolate Chips;
    White Chocolate)
Banana Cupcakes, 70
Banana Split Cups, 278
Black Bottom Cupcakes, 90
Burger Bliss, 156
Cheery Chocolate Animal Cookies,
    121
Chocolate Buttercream Frosting, 84
Chocolate-Covered Banana Pops,
    262
Chocolate Easter Baskets, 22
Chocolate Goldfish® Pretzel Clusters,
    260
Chocolate Hazelnut Cupcakes, 80
Chocolate Panini Bites, 268
Chocolate Railroad Cookies, 116
Chocolate Raspberry Panini Bites, 268

Chocolate *(continued)*
    Chocolate Sweetheart Cupcakes, 18
    Chocolate Swirl Lollipop Cookies, 182
    Classic Chocolate Cupcakes, 84
    Cookie in a Cupcake, 58
    Cupcake Sliders, 54
    Dinocakes, 4
    Double Malted Cupcakes, 96
    Fudgy Mocha Cupcakes with Chocolate Coffee Ganache, 92
    Graduation Party Cupcakes, 24
    Hanukkah Coin Cookies, 176
    Hedgehogs, 6
    Hot Chocolate Cupcakes, 62
    Indian Corn, 258
    Lollipop Flower Pots, 178
    Marshmallow Fudge Sundae Cupcakes, 56
    Marty the "Mousse," 274
    Mighty Milkshakes, 158
    Mini Dessert Burgers, 266
    Mini Mice, 2
    Mini Turtle Cupcakes, 82
    Mischievous Monkeys, 110
    Over Easy Cookies, 148
    Panda Cupcakes, 16
    Pretzel Fried Eggs, 276
    Rocky Road Cupcakes, 88
    S'more Snack Cake, 268
    S'more-Topped Cupcakes, 94
    Surprise Cookies, 192
    Tasty Turtles, 100
    Tic-Tac-Toe Cookies, 142
    Tiny Hot Fudge Sundae Cups, 146
    Treasure Chests, 128
    Zebras, 102
Chocolate Buttercream Frosting, 84
Chocolate Chips
    Cheery Chocolate Animal Cookies, 121
    Chocolate-Covered Banana Pops, 262
    Congrats Grad!, 172
    Drizzled Party Popcorn, 270

Chocolate Chips *(continued)*
    Marshmallow Chipper Cookie Cake, 180
    Mini S'mores Pies, 264
    Pretzel Fried Eggs, 276
    Rocky Road Cupcakes, 88
Chocolate-Covered Banana Pops, 262
Chocolate Easter Baskets, 22
Chocolate Goldfish® Pretzel Clusters, 260
Chocolate Hazelnut Cupcakes, 80
Chocolate Panini Bites, 268
Chocolate Railroad Cookies, 116
Chocolate Raspberry Panini Bites, 268
Chocolate Sweetheart Cupcakes, 18
Chocolate Swirl Lollipop Cookies, 182
Christmas Cookie Tree, 184
Citrus Easter Chicks, 108
Classic Chocolate Cupcakes, 84
Coconut
    Citrus Easter Chicks, 108
    Easter Nest Cookies, 166
    Mini Dessert Burgers, 266
    Sweet Snowmen, 32
Coffee
    Fudgy Mocha Cupcakes with Chocolate Coffee Ganache, 92
    Mini Tiramisu Cupcakes, 86
Colorful Caterpillar Cupcakes, 8
Congrats Grad!, 172
Cookie Dough Bears, 98
Cookie Glaze, 172
Cookie in a Cupcake, 58
Cream Cheese
    Bell Pepper Wedges with Herbed Goat Cheese, 240
    Black Bottom Cupcakes, 90
    Blueberry Cheesecake Cupcakes, 68
    Freaky Fruit Fish Bowl Cookie, 186
    Great Green Veggie Wedgies, 252
    Heavenly Ham Roll-Ups, 230
    Marty the "Mousse," 274

Crispy Bacon Sticks, 234
Croque Monsieur Bites, 210
Cupcake Cookies, 152
Cupcake Sliders, 54

D
Dinocakes, 4
Dinosaur Egg Cookies, 120
Dips & Spreads
    Hot and Spicy Hummus Dip, 230
    Hot Cheesy Chili Dip, 214
    Pound Cake Dip Sticks, 264
Double Malted Cupcakes, 96
Dragonflies, 44
Drizzled Party Popcorn, 270

E
Earth Day Delights, 164
Easter Nest Cookies, 166
Easy Easter Cupcakes, 20

F
Fairy Tale Cupcakes, 34
Fish: Tuna Schooners, 208
Fishy Friends, 10
Flip Flops, 130
Freaky Fruit Fish Bowl Cookie, 186
Friendly Face Pizzas, 258
Friendly Frogs, 36
Frosting & Glazes
    Buttercream Frosting, 8, 176
    Chocolate Buttercream Frosting, 84
    Cookie Glaze, 172
    Lemon Cookie Glaze, 108
    Maple Frosting, 30
    Powdered Sugar Glaze, 124
    Royal Icing, 122, 132, 164
Frozen Treats
    Banana Split Cups, 278
    Magic Rainbow Pops, 250
    Tiny Hot Fudge Sundae Cups, 146
Fudgy Mocha Cupcakes with Chocolate Coffee Ganache, 92

G
Go Fly a Kite Cookies, 132
Graduation Party Cupcakes, 24
Great Green Veggie Wedgies, 252
Great Zukes Pizza Bites, 236
Grilled Cheese Kabobs, 196
Guacamole Cones, 232
Guacamole Sliders, 220

H
Ham
    Bavarian Pretzel Sandwiches, 234
    California Ham Rolls, 238
    Croque Monsieur Bites, 210
    Heavenly Ham Roll-Ups, 230
Hanukkah Coin Cookies, 176
Hawaiian Pizza Bites, 196
Heavenly Ham Roll-Ups, 230
Hedgehogs, 6
Hot and Spicy Hummus Dip, 230
Hot Cheesy Chili Dip, 214
Hot Chocolate Cupcakes, 62

I
Indian Corn, 258
Italian Chicken Nuggets, 202

K
Kabobs
    Grilled Cheese Kabobs, 196
    Mini Reuben Skewers with Dipping Sauce, 224
    Poblano Pepper Kabobs, 218
Key Lime Pie Cupcakes, 66

L
Lemon
    Citrus Easter Chicks, 108
    Lemon Cookie Glaze, 108
    Lemon Meringue Cupcakes, 76
    Magic Rainbow Pops, 250
    Nothin' but Net, 140
    Pink Lemonade Cupcakes, 72
Lemon Cookie Glaze, 108

Lemon Meringue Cupcakes, 76
Liberty Bell Cookies, 168
Lime
    Key Lime Pie Cupcakes, 66
    Margarita Cupcakes, 52
Little Lamb Cakes, 14
Lollipop Flower Pots, 178

M
Mac and Cheese Mini Cups, 200
Magic Lightening Bolts, 114
Magic Number Cookies, 126
Magic Rainbow Pops, 250
Makin' Bacon Cookies, 150
Maple Frosting, 30
Margarita Cupcakes, 52
Marshmallow
    Easter Nest Cookies, 166
    Easy Easter Cupcakes, 20
    Indian Corn, 258
    Little Lamb Cakes, 14
    Marshmallow Chipper Cookie Cake,
        180
    Marshmallow Delights, 38
    Marshmallow Fudge Sundae
        Cupcakes, 56
    Marshmallow Ice Cream Cone
        Cookies, 160
    Mini S'mores Pies, 264
    Rocky Road Cupcakes, 88
    S'more Snack Cake, 268
    S'more-Topped Cupcakes, 94
    Sweet Snowmen, 32
    Sweet Sushi, 272
Marshmallow Chipper Cookie Cake,
    180
Marshmallow Delights, 38
Marshmallow Fudge Sundae Cupcakes,
    56
Marshmallow Ice Cream Cone Cookies,
    160
Marty the "Mousse," 274
Meat Loaf Cupcakes, 198
Micro Mini Stuffed Potatoes, 194
Mighty Milkshakes, 158

Mini Dessert Burgers, 266
Mini Dizzy Dogs, 202
Mini Doughnut Cupcakes, 64
Mini Mice, 2
Mini Reuben Skewers with Dipping
    Sauce, 224
Mini S'mores Pies, 264
Mini Tiramisu Cupcakes, 86
Mini Turtle Cupcakes, 82
Mint
    Angelic Cupcakes, 46
    Peppermint Pigs, 104
Mischievous Monkeys, 110
Monogram Cookies, 174

N
Noodles & Pasta: Mac and Cheese
    Mini Cups, 200
Nothin' but Net, 140
Nuts
    Chocolate-Covered Banana Pops,
        262
    Chocolate Hazelnut Cupcakes, 80
    Chocolate Panini Bites, 268
    Chocolate Raspberry Panini Bites,
        268
    Earth Day Delights, 164
    Marty the "Mousse," 274
    Mini Turtle Cupcakes, 82
    Raspberry Streusel Cupcakes, 74
    Rocky Road Cupcakes, 88
    Streusel Topping, 74
    Taffy Apple Cupcakes, 28

O
Oats
    Cookie Dough Bears, 98
    Dinosaur Egg Cookies, 120
    Meat Loaf Cupcakes, 198
Orange
    Buttercream Frosting, 8
    Chocolate Swirl Lollipop Cookies,
        182
Over Easy Cookies, 148

P

Palm Trees, 136
Panda Cupcakes, 16
Panda Pals, 106
Parmesan-Pepper Crisps, 244
Peanut Butter
  Burger Bliss, 156
  Cheery Chocolate Animal Cookies, 121
  Congrats Grad!, 172
  Drizzled Party Popcorn, 270
  Indian Corn, 258
  Peanut Butter Aliens, 118
  Peanut Butter & Jelly Cupcakes, 60
Peanut Butter Aliens, 118
Peanut Butter & Jelly Cupcakes, 60
Peppermint Pigs, 104
Pig-wich, 246
Pink Lemonade Cupcakes, 72
Pizza
  Candy Corn by the Slice, 248
  Friendly Face Pizzas, 258
  Great Zukes Pizza Bites, 236
  Hawaiian Pizza Bites, 196
Pizza Fries, 218
Poblano Pepper Kabobs, 218
Poker Night Cookies, 143
Popcorn: Drizzled Party Popcorn, 270
Pork (see also Bacon; Ham; Sausage):
  Baked Pork Buns, 222
Porky Pinwheels, 244
Potatoes
  Buffalo Wedges, 214
  Meat Loaf Cupcakes, 198
  Micro Mini Stuffed Potatoes, 194
  Pizza Fries, 218
Pound Cake Dip Sticks, 264
Powdered Sugar Glaze, 124
Prepared Dough
  Baked Pork Buns, 222
  Chili Cheese Mini Dogs, 224
  Hawaiian Pizza Bites, 196
  Mini Dizzy Dogs, 202
  Porky Pinwheels, 244

Pretty in Pink, 42
Pretzel Fried Eggs, 276
Pumpkin Spice Cupcakes, 30

R

Raspberry Streusel Cupcakes, 74
Red Velvet Cupcakes, 50
Refrigerated Cookie Dough
  Banana Split Cups, 278
  Birthday Cake Cookies, 162
  Blueberry Cheesecake Cupcakes, 68
  Building Blocks, 124
  Burger Bliss, 156
  Christmas Cookie Tree, 184
  Citrus Easter Chicks, 108
  Congrats Grad!, 172
  Cookie Dough Bears, 98
  Cookie in a Cupcake, 58
  Flip Flops, 130
  Freaky Fruit Fish Bowl Cookie, 186
  Lollipop Flower Pots, 178
  Magic Lightening Bolts, 114
  Makin' Bacon Cookies, 150
  Marshmallow Ice Cream Cone Cookies, 160
  Nothin' but Net, 140
  Over Easy Cookies, 148
  Palm Trees, 136
  Peanut Butter Aliens, 118
  Peppermint Pigs, 104
  Snickerdoodle Batter Ups, 134
  Snickerpoodles, 112
  Tiny Hot Fudge Sundae Cups, 146
  Watermelon Slices, 154
  Whirlgigs, 188
  Zebras, 102
Rice: California Ham Rolls, 238
Rocky Road Cupcakes, 88
Royal Icing, 122, 132, 164

S

Sandwiches & Sliders
  Baked Pork Buns, 222
  Bavarian Pretzel Sandwiches, 234
  Bird-wich, 254

Sandwiches & Sliders *(continued)*
    BLT Biscuits, 204
    Chocolate Panini Bites, 268
    Chocolate Raspberry Panini Bites, 268
    Croque Monsieur Bites, 210
    Grilled Cheese Kabobs, 196
    Guacamole Sliders, 220
    Mini Reuben Skewers with Dipping Sauce, 224
    Pig-wich, 246
    Sloppy Joe Sliders, 206
    Tuna Schooners, 208
    Turkey Club Biscuits, 204
Sausage & Hot Dog
    Bagel Dogs with Spicy Red Sauce, 252
    Chili Cheese Mini Dogs, 224
    Great Zukes Pizza Bites, 236
    Mini Dizzy Dogs, 202
Shellfish: Tiny Shrimp Tacos with Peach Salsa, 212
Silly Sunglasses, 144
Sloppy Joe Sliders, 206
S'more Snack Cake, 268
S'more-Topped Cupcakes, 94
Snake Snacks, 256
Snapshot Cookies, 190
Snickerdoodle Batter Ups, 134
Snickerpoodles, 112
Spicy Polenta Cheese Bites, 242
Strawberry Short Cupcakes, 78
Streusel Topping, 74
Summer Salad Lettuce Wraps, 228
Sunny Side Upcakes, 48
Surprise Cookies, 192
Surprise Package Cupcakes, 26
Swashbuckling Pirates, 122
Sweet Snowmen, 32
Sweet Sushi, 272

T
Taffy Apple Cupcakes, 28
Tasty Turtles, 100
Tic-Tac-Toe Cookies, 142

Tiny Hot Fudge Sundae Cups, 146
Tiny Shrimp Tacos with Peach Salsa, 212
Tortilla
    Great Green Veggie Wedgies, 252
    Tiny Shrimp Tacos with Peach Salsa, 212
    Tuna Schooners, 208
    Velveeta® Double-Decker Nachos, 226
Treasure Chests, 128
Tuna Schooners, 208
Turkey Club Biscuits, 204
Turtle Treats, 12

U
Under the Sea, 40

V
Velveeta® Double-Decker Nachos, 226

W
Watermelon Slices, 154
Whirlgigs, 188
White Chocolate
    Over Easy Cookies, 148
    Pretzel Fried Eggs, 276
Window-to-My-Heart Cookies, 170

Z
Zebras, 102
Zucchini: Great Zukes Pizza Bites, 236

METRIC CONVERSION CHART

VOLUME MEASUREMENTS (dry)

$1/8$ teaspoon = 0.5 mL
$1/4$ teaspoon = 1 mL
$1/2$ teaspoon = 2 mL
$3/4$ teaspoon = 4 mL
1 teaspoon = 5 mL
1 tablespoon = 15 mL
2 tablespoons = 30 mL
$1/4$ cup = 60 mL
$1/3$ cup = 75 mL
$1/2$ cup = 125 mL
$2/3$ cup = 150 mL
$3/4$ cup = 175 mL
1 cup = 250 mL
2 cups = 1 pint = 500 mL
3 cups = 750 mL
4 cups = 1 quart = 1 L

VOLUME MEASUREMENTS (fluid)

1 fluid ounce (2 tablespoons) = 30 mL
4 fluid ounces ($1/2$ cup) = 125 mL
8 fluid ounces (1 cup) = 250 mL
12 fluid ounces ($1 1/2$ cups) = 375 mL
16 fluid ounces (2 cups) = 500 mL

WEIGHTS (mass)

$1/2$ ounce = 15 g
1 ounce = 30 g
3 ounces = 90 g
4 ounces = 120 g
8 ounces = 225 g
10 ounces = 285 g
12 ounces = 360 g
16 ounces = 1 pound = 450 g

DIMENSIONS

$1/16$ inch = 2 mm
$1/8$ inch = 3 mm
$1/4$ inch = 6 mm
$1/2$ inch = 1.5 cm
$3/4$ inch = 2 cm
1 inch = 2.5 cm

OVEN TEMPERATURES

250°F = 120°C
275°F = 140°C
300°F = 150°C
325°F = 160°C
350°F = 180°C
375°F = 190°C
400°F = 200°C
425°F = 220°C
450°F = 230°C

BAKING PAN SIZES

Utensil	Size in Inches/Quarts	Metric Volume	Size in Centimeters
Baking or	$8 \times 8 \times 2$	2 L	$20 \times 20 \times 5$
Cake Pan	$9 \times 9 \times 2$	2.5 L	$23 \times 23 \times 5$
(square or	$12 \times 8 \times 2$	3 L	$30 \times 20 \times 5$
rectangular)	$13 \times 9 \times 2$	3.5 L	$33 \times 23 \times 5$
Loaf Pan	$8 \times 4 \times 3$	1.5 L	$20 \times 10 \times 7$
	$9 \times 5 \times 3$	2 L	$23 \times 13 \times 7$
Round Layer	$8 \times 1 1/2$	1.2 L	20×4
Cake Pan	$9 \times 1 1/2$	1.5 L	23×4
Pie Plate	$8 \times 1 1/4$	750 mL	20×3
	$9 \times 1 1/4$	1 L	23×3
Baking Dish	1 quart	1 L	—
or Casserole	$1 1/2$ quart	1.5 L	—
	2 quart	2 L	—